The College Application *Essay*

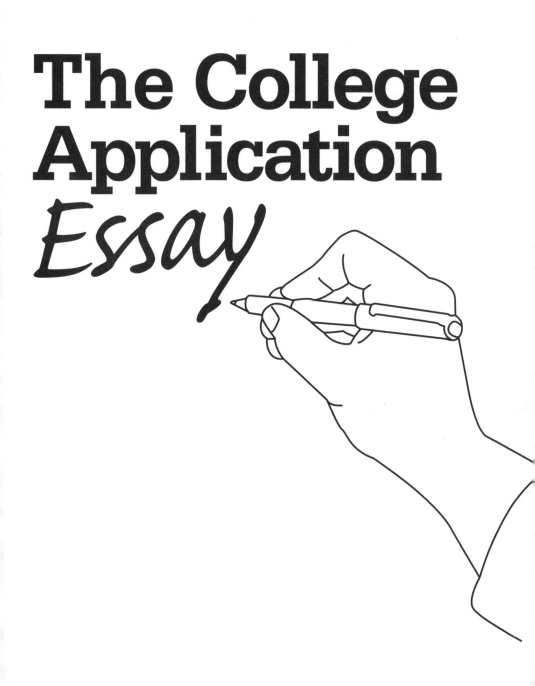

Sarah Myers McGinty

The College Application *Essay*

The College Board
New York

The College Board: Connecting Students to College Success

The College Board is a not-for-profit membership association whose mission is to connect students to college success and opportunity. Founded in 1900, the association is composed of more than 5,400 schools, colleges, universities, and other educational organizations. Each year, the College Board serves seven million students and their parents, 23,000 high schools, and 3,500 colleges through major programs and services in college admissions, guidance, assessment, financial aid, enrollment, and teaching and learning. Among its best-known programs are the SAT®, the PSAT/NMSQT®, and the Advanced Placement Program® (AP®). The College Board is committed to the principles of excellence and equity, and that commitment is embodied in all of its programs, services, activities, and concerns.

Visit the College Board on the Web: www.collegeboard.com

Copies of this book are available from your local bookseller or may be ordered from College Board Publications, P.O. Box 869010, Plano, TX 75074-0998. The price is $15.95, plus $5 for postage and handling. Purchase orders above $25 are accepted.

Editorial inquiries concerning this book should be directed to College Planning Services, The College Board, 45 Columbus Avenue, New York, New York 10023-6992.

Grateful acknowledgment is made for permission to quote from *The Poetry of Robert Frost* edited by Edward Connery Lathem. Copyright © 1923, 1969 by Holt, Rinehart and Winston. Copyright 1951 by Robert Frost. Reprinted by permission of Henry Holt and Company.

Library of Congress control number: 2004109067

ISBN-13: 978-0-87447-711-5
ISBN-10: 0-87447-711-5

10 9 8 7 6 5 4

Printed in the United States of America

Distributed by Macmillan

For Pete's sake

Contents

Acknowledgments

For anyone who has studied and taught English, writing a book is a wonderfully humbling experience. There is, of course, what Matthew Arnold called "the best that is known and thought in the world," the entire history of British and American literature, with which to compare one's effort. And then there are all the teachers, colleagues, office-mates, and mentors (including my eleventh-grade English teacher, a history teacher whose classes are said to embody the charm and wit of a good cocktail party, and a marathon-running vice principal) who have preceded me, shared with me, and inspired me. And last, there are the best teachers in the world, 20 years of high school students. Writing this book meant continual collision with something learned from someone else. I acknowledge and thank all these sources, especially my students, and most particularly my Millburn High School students. Of all who passed through room 210, it was the one in the front of the class who learned the most and had the most fun!

I also want to thank those who have guided this book to publication—first and foremost, Tom Vanderberg, Kevin Troy, Renée Gernand, and many others at the College Board—for their positive encouragement. Thanks also go to all those involved in college admissions—staffers and applicants—who shared with me their writing, their experiences, and their insights. Thanks also to NACAC and to Harvard University for their support of my research. Scott White, Tom Clifford, and Chris Meserole were essential to this project, as were the many students who made contributions to the book's samples.

Finally, I must acknowledge and thank John, J.W., Sarah, Bill, Phyllis, Dorothy, and Kim . . . they know why.

S. M. M.

A Note on the SAT® Essay

Colleges want to know you as a writer. To do this, they look at your transcripts, your application essay, and your standardized test scores, each a different piece of the puzzle. The SAT® includes a writing section with an essay. This essay is scored separately, and the results—and even the essay itself—may be part of your application. The SAT essay, however, does not take over the role of the application essay.

Why two essays? Writing assignments, both under time pressure and with the opportunity for planning, reflection, and research, have been and will continue to be part of your education: you've done this in high school, and you'll do a lot more of it in college. It's also a fair prediction that you'll do both kinds of writing in your future career: the quick e-mail versus the prepared memo or published report.

The essay portion of the SAT represents the spontaneous, "first draft" kind of writing typically required on college-level tests and examinations. You don't have complete freedom: the time and topic are limited. Evaluators look for coherence, logic, and specific evidence in support of a claim or main idea, but they do not expect to find the polish and depth of reflection that characterize the application essay.

Your application essay, on the other hand, provides an opportunity for personal narrative and the insight more typical of an editorial or memoir. While your SAT score sheds light on your ability to write quickly, succinctly, and readably about a common topic shared with other test-takers, your application essay represents writing on a topic of your choosing, prepared over time and carefully edited.

Grades in English and history, teacher recommendations, and (if requested) samples of graded academic papers add more information about your writing talents. All of these pieces—the SAT writing section, your application essay, and your teachers' assessments—fit together and contribute to the college's understanding of you as a writer.

Chapter 1
The Essay and Your Application

"Sometimes we let students write themselves in," says Thyra Briggs, dean of admission at Sarah Lawrence College. Briggs is acknowledging the importance of the essay in evaluating applicants to a college with a long tradition of attention to students' writing skills. In fact, in the 1970s, Sarah Lawrence required several essays from applicants … and two from their parents. Special attention to application essays makes sense in the context of a Sarah Lawrence education. The curriculum there is built around one-on-one meetings between professors and students, biweekly classroom work, and individual writing conferences. Of course, as at all colleges, the transcript is the primary source of information about an applicant. But after that, when admission counselors want a sense of the person behind the paper, when they are looking for the match between institution and applicant, essays can make the case. "A great essay can compensate for issues with a transcript," says Briggs, "in a way that clubs and awards might not."

Sarah Lawrence's process is its own, but it is not entirely different from that of other colleges. In most admission offices, grades and courses—the transcript—are where evaluation begins. Then other factors are taken into account: talents, recommendations, activities, testing, special circumstances, a portfolio or supplemental materials, an audition, an interview. Woven into all this is an interest in the applicant's personality and writing ability. The application essay gives colleges useful information about both these features.

Where It All Began

The application essay or personal statement has been a part of college admission since the explosion of college enrollment after World War II, evolving from direct queries like "Why in particular do you wish to attend Bates?" to more eccentric requests like "What is your favorite time of day?" (Princeton University) or "You have just published your 300-page autobiography. Please submit page 217" (University of Pennsylvania). The Reverend Mr. Bob Kinnally, the former dean of admission at Stanford University, explains the presence of the essay: "[It] helps us see and judge the depth of the [applicant's] understanding of intellectual or social issues … it also shows the quality and freshness of the applicant's mind." Although not every college requires an application essay, narrative prose figures into the admission process at a wide variety of institutions—for the 25,000 applicants to the University of Michigan, for the 8,000 applicants to Brigham Young University, for the 1,000 applicants to the Ringling School of Art and Design, for the 300 applicants to Bethel College in North Newton, Kansas. The evaluation of the essay may contribute to how a college differentiates among its top applicants. Or it may determine whether a borderline candidate has the necessary basic skills. Colleges use essays for different purposes, but essays matter—at large, small, public, private, selective, and nonselective schools.

How Colleges Read Essays

Colleges are looking to build scholarly communities, hoping to collect a population of people that likes to read and think, reflect and talk, wonder and argue. This is the mission of admissions. But as William C. Hiss, vice president for external affairs at Bates College, says, "We are often seen, wrongly, I think, as a set of intellectual gatekeepers who, like Dante's *Divine Comedy*, offer three possibilities: paradise, purgatory, or hell—that is, admit, wait-list, deny." In contrast, the colleges themselves

see a methodical and quantifiable process of selection. Dr. Marilyn McGrath Lewis, director of admission at Harvard University, describes the admission staff as a group of hard-working people "determined to bring to Harvard, students who are diverse in talents and interests." In choosing a class of first-year students, admission counselors make judgments that involve objective information (comparing two students' course loads, for example) and subjective information (a coach's opinion about how far a specific player might develop within the college's tennis program). It's what Fred Hargadon, former dean of admission at Princeton, liked to call "precision guesswork."

Making Choices

The anxiety about all this, for high school students and their families, is very real. And it's easy to start believing that the college admission process is going to be the most significant and determining feature in a young person's life. (Actually, what you do in college is more important than where you go to college.) But the "big picture" isn't a pattern of injustice and irrationality. *Both* colleges and applicants are looking and choosing. *Both* admission counselors and high school seniors are busy gathering information and making judgments based on facts and predictions. In pursuit of a common goal—the best education of the next generation of leaders and thinkers—colleges and universities, like you, will look at many options; everyone is striving to make the right choices.

Your research probably started first and you have many resources to draw upon:

- Guidance personnel and the counseling and career staff
- Web sites, catalogs, videos, and viewbooks from the colleges
- Admission counselors—at the colleges, at your high school, or at local-area information fairs
- Teachers, coaches, educational consultants, friends, parents, college graduates
- Guidebooks and data handbooks
- Campus visits and interviews
- Alumni and prior applicants from your own high school or community
- Word of mouth, general reputation, and media coverage (not the most reliable information)

You aren't doing this alone. All these resources are useful in doing your half of the choosing—deciding where to apply to college. Colleges rely on a more focused set of resources:

- Course of study
- Grades, class rank, and grade point average
- Test scores
- Biographical data (summer activities, jobs, special talents and interests)
- One or more essays, writing samples, or paragraph responses
- Support materials where appropriate (audition, tapes, portfolio)
- Recommendations
- An interview

Let's take a moment and look at how colleges make their decisions, in order to understand where the application essay fits into the picture.

The evaluation process differs at every school. Some see numerical data as the most reliable predictor of success: They look first at an applicant's grades, class rank, and test scores. California, for example, publishes eligibility minimums (grade point averages, rank, and testing) for each of its different UC campuses. Other schools try to tease from the folder a sense of an applicant's personal qualities. Julie Browning, dean of undergraduate enrollment at Rice, says, "We wonder, 'Do you have a story to tell?'" And where a school offers a distinctive program—the block plan at Colorado College, the great books curriculum at St. John's, the hands-on education of Deep Springs—application evaluation stresses the "fit" of applicant and education. All schools, even the large state universities, have a special process for the question marks—the "gray zone" applications that may require additional readers or consideration by a committee. Colleges and universities continually modify the way they evaluate folders, looking for the most reliable and the fairest way to put together a class from the limited information of an application folder.

The people who make these decisions also vary. The readers of applications are usually a combination of experienced senior admission personnel and younger staffers, often themselves recent graduates of the school. But faculty members may be part of the process. At Cal Tech, all admission decisions involve faculty. Marlboro College, University of Louisiana at Lafayette, and Reed College include student readers on admission committees. Applicants may also be looked at by specialists: music faculty hear auditions; art staff view portfolios. A dean of admission or an enrollment manager oversees everything.

The committee is not a nameless, faceless group of people, uniform in taste and attitude. It is made up of individuals. Assigned a seemingly endless pile of folders in the dark days of winter, such an audience—overworked and tired—may find that a creative, innovative, interesting, or unique element in an application makes the difference. High scores and great grades do stand out. But students mistake their audience when they visualize a stuffy bunch of academics in search of an academic superstar. Are all applications read in the same way? They can't be. And as Ted O'Neill, dean of admission at the University of Chicago, points out, "We don't want them all to be read in the same way." Similarly, Peter Van Buskirk, at Franklin & Marshall College, says,

"We're not looking for one kind of student. A liberal arts college would be ill-advised to do that." So there is no perfect applicant. Many things are sought within a class and many different elements make up the admission committee's final judgment. The folder is a web of information, a jigsaw puzzle that is interconnected and interactive. Each element plays its own part, each makes its own argument.

Your High School Record

The numbers come first. Colleges request grades, usually beginning with ninth grade. Three and a half years of performance gives them a knowledge of your academic achievement and also a look at the pattern of your growth and progress. Straight A's are nice—but rare in a challenging course of study. An improvement in grades is positive, too—the opposite will certainly raise eyebrows in the admission office. But above all other factors in the grade pattern, most colleges scrutinize the course load. A grade of B in Advanced Placement English is more important than an A in chorus. An A in chemistry carries more weight than an A in civics. Ford Stevenson, dean of admission at Brigham Young University, describes how BYU considers course choices: "We add a factor to a student's grades for a strong educational program and for more challenging courses; we will consider up to 70 percent of the applicant's program in this way." Grades, class rank, and grade point average are viewed in light of your course choices.

Grades, class rank, and grade point average are also viewed in terms of your high school and its student body. Colleges assign regional responsibility to members of the admission staff who familiarize themselves with a few states or with one part of the country. They get to know each high school and its course offerings. Some secondary schools have a reputation for excellence; others have less rigorous programs. Each school's general quality is considered in evaluating class rank and course of study.

Scores

A testing service also contributes numbers to your application. Many schools require either the SAT Reasoning Test™, some SAT Subject Tests™ , or the American College Testing Program Assessment (ACT). These standardized tests help admission personnel evaluate applicants' abilities relative to successful performance in college. The scores are seen as a yardstick with which students of widely differing backgrounds can be compared.

You probably took the PSAT/NMSQT® or practiced with books like *10 Real SATs*. Some high schools offer SAT® review courses as part of the curriculum and some students take private review courses. Familiarizing yourself with the various types of test questions can put you at ease and may make you a more efficient test-taker.

The admission committee will look at your scores and compare them to your grades. High grades can overcome low scores, but admission personnel will carefully scrutinize the course load and the high school's reputation. High scores can sometimes compensate for low grades, but

that particular combination tends to make admission personnel nervous: Does the student lack motivation? Is she just a bright goof-off?

Grades, course load, grade point average, class rank, and scores are the numerical information colleges use to evaluate an application. They look to your past as a clue to your future. Studies show that neither grades nor test scores alone indicate whether an applicant will succeed in college. However, the combination of high school record *and* scores has been found to be a fairly valid indicator of college success. College work also relies on the same study habits, self-discipline, skills, and personal qualities—enthusiasm, organization, independence of thought, responsibility, perseverance—that you need in high school. These qualities contribute to success in a career as well.

As you begin to think about college options, keep all your high school numbers in mind. Don't let yourself become overwhelmed by standardized test scores. Remember that the numbers colleges list are often the *median* scores, not the cut-off scores. If a school lists its median SAT math score as 600, then 50 percent of the class scored higher than 600, and 50 percent scored lower. Many schools now list the SAT test score range of the middle 50 percent of the freshman class. The score range of admitted students is often higher than the range for applicants, but in both cases, there are students with scores above and below the given numbers.

Numbers are only part of your application. They will, however, help you determine which schools are, for you, long shots and which are likely to be satisfied with your performance. They will help the admission committee determine if you are a sure accept, a clear deny, or a maybe.

Other sections of the application are less numerical. Warren Willingham's *Success in College: The Role of Personal Qualities and Academic Ability* (College Entrance Examination Board, 1985), showed that personal qualities are also a valid indicator of college success; many colleges look to recommendations, essays, and the interview to give them a sense of the person. And some colleges consider these elements primary criteria in an evaluation.

Recommendations

Evaluations will be written by your high school counselor and by a few of your teachers. Make these most effective by scheduling an early appointment with your counselor to discuss your college selection. If your high school is large and your relationship with your counselor a bit remote (the national ratio of students to counselors ranges between 140 to 1 and 420 to 1), you might prepare a simple life history or a résumé for your counselor. It's good preparation for filling out the applications and, by listing some of your circumstances and activities, you help your counselor write a specific and informed recommendation.

Approach your teachers early. Ask for recommendations from teachers who like you, for whom you have done well, whose courses relate to your intended area of specialization, and who are themselves articulate, careful, and responsible. You want a positive letter and one that will be consistent with the rest of your application. But don't forget that such a letter isn't likely to be written by even your favorite teacher if he or she is overworked, hassled, and pressed for time. Ask your teachers directly, "Do you have the time to write a strong recommendation letter for me for Bucknell?" Name the school, as that may influence their response. There are students a teacher would happily recommend to a less competitive school who should not expect the same enthusiasm toward an application to Stanford. And don't be downcast if the teacher says he or she is too busy or can't do it. Approach someone else. You don't want your letter gathering dust on the desk of a teacher who meant to do it but had too many periods of cafeteria duty to find the time.

You might want to give the teachers your brief résumé. They will rely mostly on what you've done in their classes, but it helps if they know you were entering piano competitions or working nights at McDonald's while you were turning out first-rate reports on Jacksonian democracy. Give the recommending teacher a list of the courses you took with him or her, the grades you received, and any special projects or major papers you did. Students come and go and most teachers appreciate a little memory-jogging. Be sure to provide stamped, addressed envelopes, and fill out all the parts of the form indicated as the student's responsibility. Waive your right of access; it shows confidence in your recommender and adds credibility to the letter. Thank-you notes at the end of the process are appropriate.

The Interview

The interview is no longer as common as the large-group information session, but if you have the opportunity, whether on campus or with a local alumni interviewer, go into an interview with a specific sense of what you want to emphasize about yourself and with a set of questions about the school that are not answered in the catalog.

Creating that résumé will help you with questions about your academic career and activities. Many of the questions are similar to those asked on the application, so you might want to look over or complete your application before beginning the interview. It helps to have one interview at a college that is courting you; you need to feel needed at about this time. Schedule the most important interview late in the sequence; you'll be more experienced and confident.

Do your "homework" and use the interviewer's knowledge of the college to help you get to know the school better. One applicant advised, "I tried to go into the interviews with an open mind and roll with the punches. But I had questions ready, too. When the alumni interviewer from Yale asked, 'Why Yale?' I asked 'Why do *you* think Yale is the place to apply? What made *you* go there?'" The better your questions, the better the impression you will make and the more useful the interview will be to you. Questions already answered in the catalog waste the interviewer's time and your time. Questions about the social life or how many students stay on campus during the weekend are better asked during the campus tour. Make your questions a little aggressive. It's much better to ask "Would you send your child to this school?" than "Do you have a major in computer science?"

The interview is a two-way street, not just an opportunity to impress the admission personnel. Don Heider, director of enrollment communications at Albright College, says, "It's the consumer's chance to see where to spend more than $100,000." Use the interview to assess further the fit between you and the school, to learn if *you* want to choose *them*.

The interview is rarely required and not every school you interview with uses the interview evaluatively. Sometimes you have only half an hour to make an impression and gather information, and the first 10 minutes is often spent getting oriented and trying to relax ("Did you find a parking place? How long a drive was it?"). Some interviewers find students too shy or guarded to be accurately assessed in a short, high-pressure meeting. Some alumni interviewers won't be able to answer all your questions, either. But take the chance, at home or on campus, and remember it's not a performance; it's a resource.

The Essay

Now for the tricky stuff. The numbers are behind you. What you've done in high school is settled. Don't expend energy or worry over things you can't change: the school you attended, the C+ you earned in English II. There are grades to be earned for the senior year and this is certainly no time to coast. But most of the numbers your high school will send to the colleges are fixed. Your recommendations are in the works. The last part of your evaluation will be drawn from the essay.

Not every college asks for an essay. But it is required on the Common Application, a form accepted by 241 colleges. And it is an option at many more schools. It may be required of transfers or the applicant applying to a special program or honors curriculum. Even two inches of white space for "Which of these activities has had the most meaning for you?" can require all the skills (and yield most of the information) of a full-length essay.

One underlying assumption made by admission offices that ask for an essay is that a student's writing will tell them something about a student's writing ability. That makes sense. Organization, usage, and correctness count. In addition, colleges believe that a student's writing will tell them something about the student's personality, thought process, values, preferences, and style. So content counts, too. Scott White, associate director of guidance at Montclair High School in New Jersey, notes, "A lot of schools really do value good writing and want to get a sense of who the student is." The essay is important both for *how* it's written and for *what* it's written about. Colleges wonder: *Can you write? Can you think?*

Colleges weigh these questions—and the essay that reflects them—with varying degrees of emphasis. Where grades in English or test scores raise questions about writing ability, the essay will be carefully reviewed. Where the transcript and support documents fail to provide a strong sense of the applicant's passions and enthusiasms, the essay may fill in the blanks. For liberal arts majors applying to Northwestern University, for example, dean and director of admission Carol Lunkenheimer says it is second only to performance in the high school course program.

Even when the essay isn't among the top three or four factors in the evaluation of an applicant, it may surface in "gray zone" cases, where a clear judgment about the applicant hasn't emerged from several reviews of the folder. Admission counselors may connect to a student who has intrigued them with thoughts about Cuban independence or missing sweat socks or Coach Rizoli; such connections can tip the balance on the last day.

Can You Write?

Combined with your English grades and some test scores, the application essay reveals your writing abilities—organization, analysis, interpretation—and your mastery of the conventions of standard written English. You'll need all this in college. As further information on the same subject, some applications require a classroom assignment. Vince Cuseo, director of admission at Occidental College, points out that a graded school paper can reveal both the writer and the "demand level" of the high school. Wheaton (MA), Middlebury, University of Vermont, and UCLA Arts are among the schools that ask for this supplementary material.

Because your ability to interpret, analyze, and express yourself clearly, correctly, and vividly will be crucial in your college courses, your college essay will be looked at in these same terms. Consider it a chance to make an important claim (in this case, a claim about yourself) and be persuasive about it. Give yourself enough time to do a thorough and careful job. Tell your own story. Don't try to sound like Albert Einstein or William Faulkner. Get some feedback in the thinking stages from a teacher, parent, or school counselor. Then polish, spell check, and proofread. Admission counselors remember—but not necessarily with affection—essays like the one that ended, "And from that day on, Daniel was my best fried."

Can You Think?

In addition, admission committees use the essay to get to know the student in a more specific and personal way than the numbers and recommendations provide. Nancy Mering, director of admission at Gordon College, says, "For us, the essay is a critical component in the application. We're looking for a special commitment and the essay gives us something the numbers don't reveal."

Nancy Siegel, a high school guidance counselor, agrees: "Colleges want a third dimension. Without the essay, the application profile is flat." Even Brigham Young University, with a fairly homogeneous applicant pool, finds diversity in the essays. The university asks applicants why they have chosen a school within the Latter-Day Saints educational system; since most applicants are members of the Church of Jesus Christ of Latter-Day Saints, one might expect a fairly uniform response, but as Ford Stevenson notes, "Although all our applicants say they want to come to BYU for the education and for the right spiritual atmosphere, this is said in many different ways. The essay can tell us about the thought process, the maturity of thinking, purposes, and goals." The application is a jigsaw puzzle; each part contributes a piece to the overall picture.

How does this work? Choice is important here. The process of choosing an answer, and often a question, is central to all college essays. Choice shows something about what and how you think. William Hiss, at Bates College, says, "The essay may help admissions see and judge the depth of the student's understanding of intellectual or social issues, but it also shows the quality and freshness of the applicant's mind." It can show priorities, values, the ability to synthesize and connect, the ability to get something out of an experience.

The essay adds a personal, human element to the application. It can breathe life into your activities, interests, experiences, or family situation, making these elements real and vivid. Nancy Donehower, a college consultant and former dean of admission at Reed College, in Portland, Oregon, says, "For me the essay is the most important part of the application. For a small college with a personal approach rather than an 'acceptability quotient,' it's the place where the kids can strut their stuff. It tells you a lot about character. It can reveal the person who likes to learn because she likes learning or the person who finds the process greater than the product. It can show how analytical the applicant is. If he says his summer in France taught him to observe cultural differences, and then says, 'For example, in France the cars are a lot smaller,' this gives a good idea of how little he's thought about and analyzed his life experiences."

The essay should not be an explanation of grades or exceptional circumstances in your background. If your grades and scores are not reflective of your ability, if your numbers don't tell all, the essay is another chance to shine. But if there are very special circumstances in your life—an illness, a family situation, a handicap—be sure to tell the college about this in a separate statement. Submit a brief account of this subject whether it's asked for or not.

The essay also shows what a student will do with an opportunity:

Did she pass it up and use a predictable, prepackaged sentiment?
"I chose X College because X is committed to learning and I want to learn."

Did he take it seriously?
Dartmouth once asked applicants to create an ideal application question and answer it; they did not learn much from questions like "Are you having a nice day?"

Did she take risks?
"These are the voyages of the Starship Nussbaum."

Did he buy it off the Internet?

Admission people can tell. And they mark the essay "DDI" when they've concluded that "Daddy did it."

The essay is particularly useful in determining the fit between the applicant and the college. Success at any school depends on knowing what you're in for; nothing is more bitter than disappointed expectations. Karen Parker, director of admission at Hampshire, says, "Looking beyond the numbers in a student's application, we want to find students who will develop the imagination and independence necessary to drive their own education. We look to the essay, the interview, and the recommendations for this information." If a college has a particular character—it's progressive or relies on a very special kind of teaching method or curriculum—the essay can reflect your understanding and enthusiasm for this special setting: the K plan at Kalamazoo College, the internship program at Northeastern, or the leadership curriculum and regimen of a service academy like the United States Military Academy at West Point, for example.

"The essay can be a powerful 'tipper' in close cases, especially with very strong or very poor essays," says Hiss.

The essay is the part of the application that most effectively personalizes your self-presentation. The recommendations are always positive, the interview is becoming less common and more a momentary "snapshot." The essay is one aspect of the application process that is open to development and is safely in *your* hands. It is an opportunity to show the admission committee a little about yourself, your insights, your enthusiasm, and your writing ability. The essay is also an opportunity to convey, under less pressure and with more preparation than the interview, something of your personal style; it counteracts the numbers and the anonymity of the application process.

Clearly, the essay adds to the overall pattern of your application. The colleges take it seriously; you should too. It is part of your need to compete and the college's need to select. If an essay is required or even allowed, use it to present yourself effectively. It is a separate part of the application and should convey information not found elsewhere. If you ignore this advice, you defeat the college's purpose in requesting an essay.

Seize this opportunity to stand out from the better numbers, the similar recommendations, the other kids. Don't default on it; don't give it away. It's a wonderful opportunity to speak out for yourself in that dark, dusty room of folders. It's not so terrible and it's not so hard. You've actually done plenty of papers like it already!

A Timeline for Applying to College

Junior Year

- Visit college fairs; talk to friends and alumni; look at various college guides; and ask counselors and teachers for suggestions.

- Talk to your parents about the finances: will you need a scholarship? A job? Loans?

- Grab an SAT testing newsprint booklet from the guidance office, ask the guidance assistant for your school's code (write that in big numerals on the front cover), and tuck it away in your desk at home for future (emergency) reference.

- Ask for viewbooks and browse online class catalogs (especially if you have an unusual or specific interest—e.g., is their psych department behavioral or humanistic? Does the linguistics department favor structural linguistics or sociolinguistics?)

- Take the PSAT/NMSQT in the fall; take SAT Subject Tests and Advanced Placement Program® Examinations at the end of appropriate courses of study.

- Meet with your school counselor and, with your parents, develop a list of colleges of interest; ask for samples of financial aid forms and local scholarship options. Look for online or school-based career or interest inventories to help you choose potential college majors or careers.

- Consider visiting colleges in the spring and over the summer; many colleges do not interview applicants until after March of their junior year.

- Mention your plans to the teachers who might write your recommendations. Start to create a brief résumé, especially if you have a special talent or extensive athletic involvement. Talk to your counselor about the NCAA Clearinghouse requirements if you want to play Division I athletics.

- Take the SAT or ACT tests in the spring.

- Keep a journal or collect interesting "important moment" articles from your reading as samples for your essay.

- Schedule a strong senior year program, emphasizing depth of program rather than a smattering of everything.

- Save some of your best class work. You might offer a paper, lab, or small portfolio to the teachers who write your recommendations.

Senior Year

September

- Focus on your classes; take the most challenging course load in which you can be successful (i.e., where you can earn B's or better), and achieve the best grades possible in your senior program.

- Meet with your guidance counselor to discuss your choices and timing; present your tentative list of colleges and ask, "What am I missing? What looks like a good match to you?"

- Attend college conferences at your high school.

- Set up campus visits and interviews; attend prospective student days and open houses at colleges of interest.

- Line up your recommending teachers.

- Download application packets from colleges that interest you.

- File the NCAA Clearinghouse forms (NCAAclearinghouse.net) if you plan to play Division I sports.

- Preregister for the CSS/Financial Aid PROFILE® if required by any of your colleges (www.collegeboard.com/css).

October

- Confirm your list of choices with your counselor. Decide if you will apply regular decision or by one of the early deadlines (see individual college options).

- Give recommending teachers the appropriate letters and enve-lopes. You may want to give them your résumé. You will definitely want to drop them a thank-you note after the deadlines.

- Take the SAT Reasoning Test and/or SAT Subject Tests. Enter the numerical codes for the colleges you are applying to.

- Write for paper copies of application forms if you cannot download them. Pool application essay questions by type (see Chapter 4); begin thinking about the questions. Group schools that accept the Common Application together but look carefully on the Web site (www.commonapp.org) for required supplements.

- Research scholarships that may apply to you; talk to your parents about the finances again.

- If applying Early Decision or to a college with rolling admission, start writing your application and essay (see Chapter 5).

- Complete any rolling admissions applications, particularly to those state institutions that require only a transcript, an application form, and test scores.

November

- Get Free Application for Federal Student Aid (FAFSA) forms from your guidance counselor. Your parents can fill out the FAFSA online at www.fafsa.ed.gov.

- Finish SAT Reasoning Test and/or SAT Subject Tests testing.

- Early Decision deadlines are often November 1 or 15. Remember that, in most cases, you can make only one Early Decision application.

- If you are applying Regular Decision, begin filling out applications (either paper copies or online) and writing essays (see Chapter 5). Your deadlines will fall between December 1 and February 15.

December

- Complete essays. You can download applications from assorted software programs or use the forms the colleges provide. You can, in many cases, apply entirely online.

- Proofread everything TWICE! Make a checklist to be sure you've had scores sent, enclosed checks, and notified your counselor about each school you're applying to. Mail applications early. Verify receipt of online material.

January–March

- Follow up on any missing details; continue to mail or submit applications according to the deadlines.

- Focus on producing a solid senior record; it's your last chance to "rule the school."

- Continue to visit or interview if you missed a school of interest; it's best to see a college when classes are in session. Schools with rolling admission may accept applicants well into the spring.

- Prepare and file financial aid forms (www.FAFSA.ed.gov) and other scholarship applications.

April–June

- When your letters come through, expect at least one rejection. It's probably going to be part of the process somewhere along the way, and it only shows you've measured correctly the full range of your own possibilities.

- Don't run down the halls shouting, "I got in." If you want to celebrate, make it a private affair.

- Revisit the colleges that have admitted you and that are "finalists" on your list. Touring a school when you know you can enroll there is very enlightening. Ask yourself, "Is this where I want to take my talents and charms? Can these people be my friends?"

- Choose one school and make your deposit before the universal reply date of May 1. If you choose to remain on a waiting list, send a letter expressing your interest and any new information that might strengthen your case.

- Get a summer job that pays good money.

- Go to the prom, even if you have to go with your cousin.

Sometimes I think students devote their senior summer to making home a place they are willing to leave. Try to remember, somewhere along the way, to thank your parents for all they've done for you; recognize that the big scary change in your life is mirrored by a big scary change in theirs.

Chapter 2

What You Know About Essay Writing

A New but Familiar Assignment

When the application packets begin to arrive, the anxiety builds. It was fun looking at the photographs, reading the course offerings, and fantasizing about next fall. But the burden of choice is shifting from the schools you choose to the schools that will choose you.

As described in Chapter 1, much of the data for this decision is settled. Grades have been recorded, scores reported, recommendation letters provided. But the essay is yet to be written. The application you're filling out may ask for a list of the items you'd include in a time capsule or perhaps you've been asked to describe lunch with a famous person. Even a straightforward essay about yourself may seem intimidating; it may seem as if you've never done anything like this before. Your teachers assigned papers and reports, with topics such as the theme of love in a particular novel or the causes of a given war. This seems to be a very different business.

But think about it for a moment and you'll realize that you have, in fact, done this assignment before—*many* times. All those papers for English class—and for history, and even for science—were essentially like the college essay. And even if the college essay seems harder, it isn't. It's just different—and in many ways it's easier.

The Challenge of the College Essay

As you have seen in the first chapter, the essay is a special opportunity to introduce yourself. You have an attentive audience that believes this part of your application will give useful additional information, a different and reliable lens on you. And although the admission committee will not choose or reject you on the basis of this single element, the essay can be a strong voice in your favor, a way to stand out from the rest, a determining factor for a "gray zone" application. According to Audrey Smith, dean of enrollment at Smith College, "We'll take a risk for the right reason." Sometimes it is the essay that gives them that reason. So while admission people want to hear from your high school counselors and teachers, they also want to hear from you.

The college essay should be, in one way or another, an essay of self-analysis. Self-analysis is not easy and it can be especially hard to do at this point in your life, when many of your goals and plans are unsettled. You may already have confronted this problem at the interviews. Admission people ask, "Tell us about yourself" or "What are your hopes and aspirations?" These are questions that require self-analysis, and they're pretty hard. The college has questions about you partly because you still have questions about yourself. But the essay is a chance to demonstrate which questions you've asked yourself and what answers you've found.

The college, then, is asking you to do something genuinely difficult—tell about yourself—and here the pressure is really on. The audience is critical and crucial; readers unknown to you intend to take your performance seriously.

The essay is also going to be examined as a clue to your writing ability. Columbia University lets you know what they're looking for right on the application: "Please remember that we are concerned not only with the substance of your prose but with your writing style as well." Andrew Stewart, a history teacher at Pattonville High School in Missouri, sees wisdom in this strategy: "Of course the essay is seen as an index to student writing. After all, a very large part of your performance and evaluation in college will be based on essays and written tests. Skill in essay writing is essential to success in a competitive liberal arts college. The essay portion of the application is one way to find out if prospective students have mastered the basic skills they'll need when they're there." Carol Lunkenheimer, at Northwestern, sees the essay as a useful defense of a student's acceptability. "It is greatly in an applicant's favor if the reader can say, 'This kid can write.'"

So the challenge is to have your own say with power and precision. *You* in one page! Clearly there is pressure here, and it is natural for anything that is challenging to be a little threatening. But with yourself as the subject, you actually have all it takes to succeed!

The Structure

A college essay is nothing new; it is the type of writing with which you are most familiar. Let's look at your writing skills and the kind of writing you have learned in the last 12 years.

First of all, it was organized—your paper on *The Great Gatsby* had a format, as did your papers for history and science. They had a beginning, a middle, and an end. You did not just ramble. You focused on a single point and stuck to it, describing and developing your insights and observations. At the end, you returned to your main idea, which you summarized and refocused.

A paragraph on the economic causes of the Civil War might have looked like this:

> Beginning: Some of the causes of the Civil War were economic
> Middle: A sentence or two on Northern prosperity
> A sentence or two on Southern agricultural economy
> Three or four sentences on the conflicts these
> different economies created in trade, standard of
> living, and relations with England
> End: A concluding sentence

A paper on *The Great Gatsby* might have looked like this:

> Beginning: *The Great Gatsby* explores different kinds of love
> Middle:
>> A paragraph about friendship
>>> Daisy and Jordan
>>> Gatsby and Nick
>> A paragraph about false love
>>> Nick and Jordan
>>> Myrtle and Tom
>> A paragraph about true love
>>> Gatsby and Daisy
> End: Summary/conclusion

A science paper might have followed this plan:

> Main idea: Desert animals show a significant adaptation to their environment
> Body:
>> A paragraph about adjustment to heat/cold:
>>> burrowing animals
>>> cold-blooded animals
>> A paragraph about adjustment to weather:
>>> natural protections from sandstorms
>>> natural protections from dehydration
>> A paragraph about adjustment to limited food:
>>> storing nourishment
>>> extracting water
> Conclusion: A summary or conclusion drawn from the above

The structure of formal writing has been described in this way:

> Tell 'em what you're gonna tell 'em
> Tell 'em
> Tell 'em what you told 'em

This is a good way to think of your writing. The three parts are a natural way to present any topic. After all, you are leading the reader along an unfamiliar path. You have to give that reader an idea of the basic subject so she can focus her attention. The middle will be meaningful if she's got a focus to follow; she can keep an eye out for love or economic factors. Likewise, with a reiteration or closing comment at the end, you strengthen the coherence of your argument.

You've used this three-part pattern in a variety of situations.

The paragraph	The essay
Topic sentence	Introduction
Development	Body
End sentence	Conclusion

No matter what your writing background, you have worked with this common structural pattern. It has been part of your school curriculum for a number of years, and it is something you have practiced. It is a skill that seems to come naturally to most writers when they want to explain something or describe an idea unfamiliar to their readers. Even work on the school newspaper or personal writing may have given you practice in this three-part format:

Dear Joe,
My summer vacation rocked.
Here is what we did [the trip, my driving test,
the mall, etc.] ...
It was really the best.
Love,
Jennifer

You have been taught this structure, and it is just what you need for the college essay. (Sample 4 in Chapter 7 is a good example.) It is also the underlying structure of a lot of college writing, business writing, journal articles, proposals, reports, and speeches. If you're a bit shaky about how it works, pay careful attention to Chapter 3, Writing an Essay, because you'll need this skill now *and later*.

The Style

You're experienced with the structure you'll need for the essay, and there's more good news: You have also had 12 years of writing practice. You know the difference between academic and personal writing, between term papers and diaries, between essays and love letters.

Everyone has a natural storehouse of different styles of speech and of writing. You talk to the person taking your order at the local pizza parlor with a very different vocabulary and style than you would use if a corporate receptionist asked, "May I help you?" So you automatically write for each assignment in a different way. Without being conscious of it, you use a style and vocabulary for a paper on *Hamlet* that is nothing like what you'd use in writing a note to Mom. You know when you have to check your spelling and you automatically strive for the level of vocabulary and correctness suitable for each piece of work.

> In his tragic play *Hamlet, Prince of Denmark*, Shakespeare presents a character totally buggin' over his father's death.

Whoops! The humor is a result of mismatching style and situation. Most writers move back and forth between various levels of language and styles of writing as easily as they adapt their speech to their listeners. You know the right level of language for a given situation and you know the college essay is a serious piece of writing. But it is not as formal as most school writing; you'll want all the clarity and correctness you can produce but, considering the subject (you), you'll also want a more direct and personal tone than you might otherwise use. A conversational tone is best. Susan Paton, college counselor at the Hopkins School in Connecticut, says, "We encourage students to use their natural voice and forget the five-dollar words." Spelling and sentence structure should be correct but your word choice and style should not be heavily academic, full of thesaurus words, or unnatural.

You have a good idea of what your strengths and weaknesses are as a writer. (For a fresh look, browse through your writing folder from last semester, or ask your English teacher.) You have plenty of time to proofread, look up potential problem words, and edit your essay. Any flow of good ideas can be interrupted by dum errers; save time to proofread thoroughly and correct your own dumb errors.

You certainly have adequate motivation built into this situation. It's only a matter of diligence to bring your performance to perfection and, again, you've had 12 years of practice.

The Subject

The greatest strength you bring to this essay is 17 years or so of familiarity with the topic: YOU. The form and style are very familiar, and best of all, you are the world-class expert on the subject: YOU.

You know a lot about you. If you can write about wars, novels, experiments, and sonnets, writing about yourself should be simple. You don't have to do any research. You don't have to study the major city-states of the Renaissance or read *Macbeth*. You already know all you need to know. And there is a wealth of information, thousands of incidents, events, and facts, from which to draw. Instead of being at a loss for material, you may find the quantity a little overwhelming. However, you don't have to despair of finding a topic; it has been the subject of your close scrutiny every morning since you were tall enough to see into the bathroom mirror.

Another wonderful aspect of this topic is that no one else has it; it is unique. No essay will directly compete with yours. You've picked colleges that are appropriate for you, probably a group of similar schools that include a "long shot" and a "sure thing." They are tailored to you and you are, therefore, tailored to them. Your desires, plans, and abilities probably fall within a profile of each college's student body, so your essay has every reason to stand up to the other submissions.

Remember, the colleges are not looking for a single answer. Admission personnel do not look for a specific student. There is no set combination of items that every applicant must have to gain acceptance at a certain college. You, your essay, and your application profile do not have to match a single narrow standard. They need only fit into one of the constituencies, into the larger pattern of students at your chosen school.

The best part of the college essay is that it can't be wrong. One of my students wrote an entire paper on "The Love Song of J. Alfred Prufrock" as if it were a poem set in an aquarium. It turned out she had read the line about the yellow fog and thought it was "the yellow frog" that pressed its nose against the windowpane! But had she said she loved aquariums, who could possibly question that? Everyone laughed at the boy who thought "On First Looking into Chapman's Homer" was about baseball, but an essay on an imagined lunch with Babe Ruth would be a different story. Follow the advice of Thyra Briggs, dean of admission at Sarah Lawrence College: "Take a deep breath, relax, and believe in yourself." There is no fixed critical opinion about you, no standard theory of interpretation. You can't come off looking bad because you didn't know that Richard Wright was a Communist, that Hamlet's problem was melancholia, that "Stopping by Woods on a Snowy Evening" is about suicide. You don't have to do research. You have had lots of experience with this "text" and you are the major authority in the field.

The topic may seem hard, but it's really the essay's greatest attraction. It's about you—a topic you know, need to know, want to talk about, have as your exclusive territory, and can't be wrong about. You are the real expert and can easily speak with both authority and conviction.

The Process

Finally, the process of all school papers is the process you will use, and not only as far as the steps to follow. Of course, you will want to brainstorm a little, organize a lot, write, rewrite, and edit. Chapter 3 is a guide to the composition process. But the thought process is the same as well: focus and prove.

Let's look back at that paper on *The Great Gatsby*. You chose or were assigned a topic: love. You narrowed it down to a manageable size: three major points. Then you explored the novel and drew out the incidents that proved Fitzgerald portrayed different kinds of love. You gathered as many examples as made your point vivid and then described them to the extent that they supported your theme.

The application of this process to the college essay is simple. In this case, you look into your life, select an aspect of yourself that you see as a strength, a personal characteristic like commitment or creativity or resilience, one that may not come through in the rest of your application's facts, grades, and numbers. Then you'll find the substantiating evidence—an event, experience, or incident—that reveals this aspect. Determination? How about four years riding the bench for junior varsity soccer. Insight? Maybe that growing understanding that friends who say, "I'll save you a seat" and then forget to save you a seat aren't really friends. *You* are the starting point. *Events* are the evidence. That fateful summer, that wonderful biology class, that job at the pizza place isn't worth much in itself. Each one is valuable only as a lens into your thought process, your way of doing things, your choices and values.

Thus the standard school essay is good preparation for writing a college essay. Academic topics aren't so far from college essay topics. Both are often based on the isolation of a single aspect of some dense and complex phenomenon. A war, a novel, a food chain may be good for a day's lesson. But these are too much for an essay topic, and *so are you*. No teacher has asked you to write on a topic like, "Tell me everything you know about Napoleon"; the college doesn't want to hear all about you either. Avoid a sort of shotgun approach; telling everything about yourself is not the idea. Select *one* thing about yourself and illuminate that. The light from one interesting point will reflect a lot about your entire personality. Less is more here. A small and interesting facet will shine most brightly.

The idea is not so much to be different or noble or scholarly. Scott White, at Montclair High School, says, "You don't have to write like Hemingway." But do try to be vivid and clear. What you want to show is your intensity, enthusiasm, insight, and understanding. This is, after all, what the college wants to see. It's what they hope to measure in the essay and what you'll need to succeed when you're accepted.

Don't panic. You have all the skills you need and the assignment is your best and favorite topic. Your school essays have been your training ground for structure and process. The next chapter will take you step-by-step through the process of writing an essay. Chapters 4 and 5 offer sample college essay questions and some strategies for making the most of this special essay. However you approach it, keep in mind that your essay is your own exciting opportunity to introduce yourself to a college.

A Timeline for Application Essays and Personal Statements

Junior Year

- Listen to the seniors complain about the essays … but not too much. You'll have everything you need when the time comes.

- Commit yourself to doing well on the writing assignments given in your history and English classes. These skills will help you with application essays and with future college writing.

- Consider keeping a journal or an "idea bank" of thoughts, reflections, and important conversations from which you can later draw inspiration. Definitely keep some sort of diary if you go on a college visitation trip.

- Ask your English teacher if you can write a personal essay for a class assignment (writing practice is a good thing, and your English teacher knows a lot about writing).

Senior Year

September and October

- Look at the questions on sample applications and on the Common Application. Begin to think about possible answers.

- Float some ideas past your teachers and guidance counselors and ask for their reactions.

- Talk to your parents. Ask them what they consider to be your strengths and talents.

- Make a list of factors, abilities, and characteristics that would recommend you for inclusion in any group. Think about which of these will already be apparent from your application. (Example: You may have a long history of involvement with tennis, but your win-loss record and ranking will be in your application. If you want to write about tennis, your essay should be about determination or resilience or adaptability ["My Annoying Doubles Partner"] rather than factual information found elsewhere).

- If you are applying Early Decision, start drafting.

November and December

- Continue to ask yourself questions about your interests and abilities. Choose events or information that reflect those features of your personality. Don't write about something you thought about for the first time an hour ago. Don't try to write about something "no one has ever written about before."

- Focus on what you've thought, not what you've done or where you've been.

- Ask for intervention or guidance from a teacher, parent, or counselor well before you consider yourself to be "done." It's hard to accept criticism or advice if you believe you're finished.

- Write an essay.

- Now write another one (throw the first one away if you tried to tell them what they wanted to hear—you don't know what they want to hear).

- Put it all away for a few days; think about what you've written and then revise. Consider crossing out the first paragraph of your essay for a faster, more focused beginning.

- PROOFREAD.

- Keep copies of your essays and attach the originals (or handwrite them) onto the applications.

- PROOFREAD.

- If you apply Early Decision and end up making additional applications at the end of December, take a second look at the essay you threw together in October and be sure it's the best you can do.

- Mail and relax: with Lorene Cary, in her memoir *Black Ice*, say, "I wrote as prettily as I could and dared them not to like it."

Chapter 3
Writing an Essay

$\mathbf{T}$he purpose of this chapter is to review the process of writing any essay. You may be experienced enough with this form to skim this chapter quickly and go right on to Chapters 4 and 5, which apply the general form to the application essay. Check the summary section at the end of this chapter. If the concepts there seem unfamiliar, or if writing has not been your strength in high school, you will want to read and study this chapter carefully before writing the essays for your applications and again when you begin writing essays in college.

What Exactly Is an Essay?

Essays are as diverse as writers themselves and do not conform to as specific a pattern as sonnets or tragedies or lab reports. However, most essays are some sort of a defense of a writer's opinion or point of view. The opinions vary greatly: Shakespeare's plays all deal with the restoration of order; Springfield ought to build a youth activity center; the United States should no longer invest its tax monies in manned space exploration; gerbils need a stable social environment to flourish.

Personal and particular or academic and abstract, the essay tries to convince the reader that an opinion, theory, claim, or interpretation is correct. Thus an essay can be a newspaper editorial advocating reduced taxes, a term paper on *The Color Purple* as a classical tragedy, a proposal from an architectural firm for a shopping mall, or a defense of an innocent client in a court of law. The college essay, too, presents a thesis—a view of the applicant—to the college admission board, and persuades them of its validity.

Writing any essay is a process. There are stages and steps to follow. The writer who makes multiple drafts and the one who rarely revises both go through a similar process, either on paper or in their heads. But like Abraham Lincoln, who scribbled a few notes on an envelope on his way to Gettysburg, most writers prefer to complete some of the preliminary steps on paper. The process is:

1. Preparation and prewriting
2. A number of drafts (from one to several)
3. Revising and editing

A 45-minute final examination essay in modern European history might involve:

1. Two minutes of preparation
2. Forty minutes on the single draft you will write
3. Three minutes of quick proofreading and revising

The final essay or term paper for the same course would involve:

1. A few days of planning and preparation, with research in the library
2. Two drafts or more
3. Editing and revising; optional review by another reader—a friend, teacher, or peer tutor at your school's writing center

The examination essay takes less than an hour; the term paper, one to two weeks. However, the three-part process is used in both writing situations.

Prewriting

The goal of prewriting is to develop your focus; it has four aspects:

1. Brainstorming
2. Asking Questions
3. Focusing
4. Organizing

Brainstorming

It's time to clean your room. Throw everything that's not nailed down into a heap in the center: books, clothes, CDs, letters, used coffee cups, that paper plate with its little scabs of pizza sauce. Now you have a sense of how much you have to do and exactly with what you have to work. Piles can be sorted from the central mess—one for the laundry, one to be saved, one to go in the trash, and so on. Many writers begin with a similar fast and disorganized collection of potential ideas. They throw every possibility onto a list or pile of note cards and then look at the result. Patterns, groups, and an overall sense of what they have to work with begin to emerge. This is brainstorming.

Grab a piece of paper or sit down at a computer. Write the limits of your assignment on the top of the page: 750 words on my summer vacation, a paragraph on the importance of the National Labor Relations Act, a three- to five-page paper on Emily Dickinson, a ten-page paper on cloning. Now write down everything you can think of that relates to the topic. List single words that pop into your mind. Ask yourself questions about the topic, make statements, wonder, speculate, recall, and connect. Set a timer or otherwise establish a time limit so that you will keep on writing for several minutes. Do not stop to daydream or reread. Just write, write, write.

Here are two different samples of students' three-minute brainstorms on *The Simpsons*.

Sample 1

I love *The Simpsons*—everyone watches it—people say "D'oh!" now like Homer, the American 'Everyman'—they live in a little town, Springfield, but it has everything (nuclear power plant, airport, desert)—they all look yellow—I love the episode about the trillion dollar bill, when Homer has to get it back but Castro steals it—and the ones about who shot Mr. Burns—Homer lives for beer and donuts and television—a working class American family, the challenges—I know about 20 episodes by heart—is that normal?

(This student jotted down a stream-of-consciousness response of his personal feelings about the topic.)

Sample 2

A cartoon sitcom
Created by Matt Groening; now written by a team
Maggie is perpetually one year old
Lisa is always in the second grade; Bart is in fourth grade
Bart's best friend is Milhouse
Bart likes to prank-call Moe
Mr. Burns owns the nuclear power plant
Homer is always falling asleep at work
The Simpsons' cat is named Snowball 2—who was Snowball 1?
Most of the shows divide into three sub-episodes
They emphasize family a lot—love but also conflicts (sisters-in-law, Grampa)
Apu runs the convenience store
The Flanders live next door—very religious
Lots of guest appearances—Bob Hope, Mel Gibson, Jay Leno, U2, Lisa Kudrow
Sideshow Bob was Krusty the Clown's sidekick, but now it's Sideshow Mel

They criticize big companies: time shares, Microsoft, NASA,
SUV's, the tomacco
Marge has blue hair and older twin sisters
Maggie costs $847.63 in the opening credit
They go to Reverend Lovejoy's church
They often tackle theology—God even appears—and great lit-
erature (*Hamlet*, Maya Angelou, Edgar Allan Poe, Amy Tan)

(This student is more knowledgeable about the topic; she produced a more expansive and connected list of thoughts.)

This stream-of-consciousness collecting process doesn't require a keyboard or even paper and pencil. Some writers mull over an idea for days or weeks or even years. But a significant percentage of writers use a journal, diary, or notebook: they write as a way to begin thinking about writing. Nathaniel Hawthorne, for one, kept such a journal:

The life of a woman, who, by the old colony law, was
condemned always to wear the letter A, sewed on her
garment, in token of her having committed adultery.

The beginning of *The Scarlet Letter*, and quite a few other Hawthorne stories, can be traced to the brainstorming he did in this journal. So, for many writing assignments, the way to begin (especially if beginning is difficult and you aren't sure where to begin) is to brainstorm thoughts and responses to the assignment and see exactly with what you have to work. This can be a quick preparation for writing (as for a final examination) or, if you have the luxury of time, you can add to your brainstorm and collect ideas for quite a while before you go on to the next step.

Asking Questions

After you have discovered that you do, in fact, know something about your subject, that you do have thoughts about it, go over your notes and jottings, ask questions, and look for repetitions or connectable ideas. You are moving toward a focus. In the second *Simpsons* example, there is a mix of themes and facts about the show. A few of the facts are about the show itself, but most have to do with characters in the Simpsons' immediate family or various supporting characters; almost all relate to other items on the list.

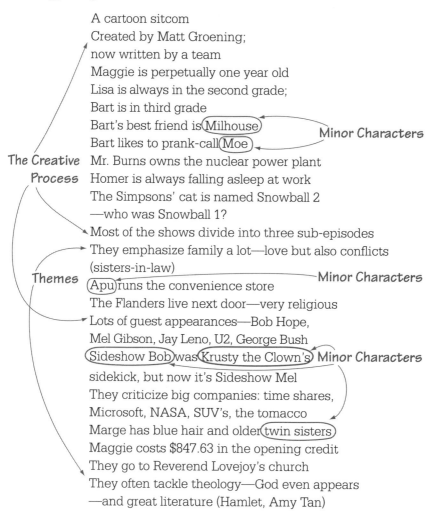

A cartoon sitcom
Created by Matt Groening;
now written by a team
Maggie is perpetually one year old
Lisa is always in the second grade;
Bart is in third grade
Bart's best friend is Milhouse — Minor Characters
Bart likes to prank-call Moe
Mr. Burns owns the nuclear power plant
Homer is always falling asleep at work
The Simpsons' cat is named Snowball 2
—who was Snowball 1?
Most of the shows divide into three sub-episodes
They emphasize family a lot—love but also conflicts
(sisters-in-law)
Apu runs the convenience store — Minor Characters
The Flanders live next door—very religious
Lots of guest appearances—Bob Hope,
Mel Gibson, Jay Leno, U2, George Bush
Sideshow Bob was Krusty the Clown's Minor Characters
sidekick, but now it's Sideshow Mel
They criticize big companies: time shares,
Microsoft, NASA, SUV's, the tomacco
Marge has blue hair and older twin sisters
Maggie costs $847.63 in the opening credit
They go to Reverend Lovejoy's church
They often tackle theology—God even appears
—and great literature (Hamlet, Amy Tan)

The Creative Process

Themes

Any one of these could lead to a topic and then to a thesis for an essay.

Go over your notes several times, adding any new ideas that come to you. Look for themes or patterns among the items you've listed. Most importantly, ask yourself questions:

- Why do the characters never grow older?
- Is family presented as a good thing or a source of conflict?
- Why is *The Simpsons* so popular?
- What makes *The Simpsons* so funny … to adults and to kids?
- Is Homer Simpson a brief fad or a more important comment on culture?
- Do girls like *The Simpsons* as much as boys?
- Is Marge the voice of reason?
- Are women presented more positively than men?
- Can a cartoon be both humorous *and* serious?
- What are the connecting ideas that run through the series?

What you are doing now is analyzing your topic, breaking it down into pieces. *The Simpsons* is too big a topic for an essay; better to concentrate on one element of its popularity, its humor, or its production. This principle is familiar from your school assignments, as well: an essay for English might focus on one element of a poem: form, language, setting, tone, theme. A history essay on a president might focus on one campaign strategy, one conflict with Congress, one area of policy. A college application essay might focus on one job, one experience, one aspect of your personality. Getting at a worthwhile aspect begins with questions:

- Why is this important?
- What is the purpose or function of this one element?
- Why did this occur?
- What was the impact of this one event, decision, scene, choice?
- What evidence can I give of the further importance or impact of this?

All kinds of questions can lead to topics and move you toward a focus and a plan.

Focusing

You need to get down to work now. Your essay must prove a single claim or thesis.

If this is a 45-minute midterm, latch onto the first topic that jumps off the page and get to the writing as quickly as possible. If this is an out-of-class essay, you need to develop your own thesis. You will shift and adjust this thesis as you work on other parts of your essay, but one angle or aspect of a large and complex topic is your beginning. Look at the groups and clusters of ideas you have come up with and try making statements about some of them.

- *The Simpsons* is successful because it appeals to both adults and kids.
- *The Simpsons* explores complicated issues such as materialism, God, death, prejudice, and morality.
- The Simpsons as a family are endearing because of their faults.

These are preliminary thesis statements and any one of them is a good start: each focuses on an aspect of *The Simpsons* and asserts an opinion or claim about the show.

One interesting sentence can be the basis of a persuasive argument. From the groups of ideas on the brainstorm sheet and the questions you've asked yourself, make your own list of possible thesis statements. If time allows, consult with your teacher or professor about these possible topics. If a full-length research paper is the assignment, a trip to the library's databases, reader's guides, and indexes in the field might supplement the brainstorming process and help you narrow down and select a topic. Choose the topic that most interests you, the topic about which you have the most to say, the most specific topic you can devise; then get on to the business of making a simple plan.

Organizing

You have chosen a focus; you have a tentative thesis statement. Now you need a plan of attack. You probably are not ready to create a final outline, but it is wise to impose a little order at this point. You need to determine how you will prove your claim.

Revise your brainstorm sheet and eliminate ideas unrelated to your topic. It may be painful to cross items out, but you can't include everything. A paper that includes *everything* is not an essay; it's still just a brainstorm. Some students write everything they know and hope the teacher will hunt through it and find what he or she wants! Better to prove a small point than require the *reader* to find the meaning in a jumble of information. Take out the red pen and start cutting.

If time and the assignment dictate, you should research your topic. Reread the primary source material, consult critical sources, talk again with your teacher. Begin to line up possible evidence to support your proposed thesis statement.

Once you are satisfied that you have adequate information, rearrange your brainstorm sheet into a tentative list of points or supporting ideas for your topic. Here are three samples of early organizational efforts that include a preliminary thesis and a general plan of proof to be covered in the essay:

Shakespeare's plays deal with the restoration of order

1. *Romeo and Juliet:* the conflict between the Capulets and the Montagues must give way to peace and order
2. *The Taming of the Shrew:* Kate's aggressive attempts to dominate men must yield to a more orderly and peaceful relationship between men and women
3. *Hamlet:* Hamlet's burden is the ghost's command that he restore order by avenging his father's murder

Gerbils need a stable social environment to flourish

1. The control group
   a. eating habits
   b. growth
   c. behavior
   d. mating habits
2. The experimental group
   a. eating habits
   b. growth
   c. behavior
   d. mating habits

The *Simpsons* is a serious cartoon
  Adult world of work/life in suburbia
  Money and business themes
  Good and evil—serious issues
  The world the way children see it

As you create a simple outline, choose an appropriate order for your points. One common organizational plan is by time: Discuss a process step by step, the events in a novel in the order in which they happened, the plays of Shakespeare in the order in which they were written.

The most useful order of points in an essay is from least to most important. Remember that the goal of an essay is to persuade. It is therefore logical to begin small and build toward your most convincing argument. When you borrow money from your parents, you mention how responsible you've been recently, your good grades last semester, and other things that set the stage. But your big persuasions—your safe driving record, your plan to fill the car with gas, how desperately you need it—come at the end. You don't start big then fade; you tuck in any tenuous ideas early on and save up for the grand finale.

The same principle applies to writing. The writer of the essay on *The Simpsons* looks over the four ideas: Springfield, money, good/evil, and family. She continues to ask questions: What do I mean by serious? Serious to whom? Can a cartoon be serious? What are cartoons, anyway—are they the same as other art, but just graphically different? What makes *The Simpsons* serious? Whose world is this? She refines her claim or thesis and then revises her ideas, regroups, and builds her argument toward the most persuasive point. The final plan might look something like this:

Thesis: *The Simpsons* seems like an adult cartoon, but it is really a child's world that's depicted.

1. *The Simpsons* has many elements of serious, adult entertainment
   a. The universal suburban town: Springfield (there are Springfields in NJ, MA, IL, etc.)

   b. Life in the suburbs: house on a street, the mall, driving everywhere, school, local bar

c. Themes of family life: the kids (gambling the Christmas money), Grampa, sisters-in-law

d. Money and business: Mr. Burns as embodiment of capitalistic excess, no one ever pays the tab at Moe's, Apu working his way into American society, Homer's crazy schemes (selling grease; the tomacco)

e. Social criticism: violence on TV ("Itchy and Scratchy"), corporate corruption, public versus private schools

2. But the show appeals to children because it's an ideal child's world

a. Springfield seems to be the whole world: dam, airport, Civil War cemetery—all-purpose town

b. Family is focused mostly on the children (Lisa's school choice, Bart's homework)

c. Work is pointless or corrupt: Homer sleeps or schemes, Burns exploits workers

d. Adults are unreliable, out of touch with reality, likely to make mistakes (Principal Skinner, Ned Flanders, Moe)

e. Everything bad is temporary—crashed cars, broken arms, the house demolished in a town's revenge are only temporary calamities, cured or corrected in the next episode

f. Children are wise (Lisa—college applications, solving the mystery, saving the day) or at least wiseguys (Bart)

Conclusion: no one ever ages on *The Simpsons* because it is meant to be a world ruled by children.

Since the first section of this essay offers an interpretation that is rejected by the second section, the organization is established by the thesis: What you might think, followed by what you should think.

This organizing process is not a substitute for the final outline you need for a 15-page research paper, but it is an adequate preparation for most short essays or essay test answers and a necessary first step if such a final outline is required.

Getting the Most Out of Prewriting

The prewriting process can take you from the bewilderment of having just received an assignment to confidence in being ready to write. Use it as much as you need. You may brainstorm and organize a test answer in a total of five minutes, or mull over ideas for weeks, brainstorming three or four times, and then sitting down to compose a final outline. Most writers need some help and preparation; they gather their ideas together in a *brainstorm,* sort and group them, ask *questions* about their first thoughts, *focus* on a tentative thesis, and then *organize* their proof in a logical pattern.

Drafting

The next step is to begin writing. Complete the research and rereading of sources; continue to ask questions, refine, and regroup your ideas. Then begin to write your essay in these three parts: introduction, body, conclusion. Although the three parts work together, they need to be thought of separately. The introduction and conclusion are necessary frames for the real substance of your essay, the body. Like the bread in a sandwich, the introduction and conclusion keep everything neat, organized, and together. In between lies the important business, the evidence or proof itself. All three parts make the whole.

The Introduction

There are essentially two strategies for an introduction. One is to provide the reader with a road map for the area about to be covered. This is especially helpful if the territory is tricky or the journey is long, as with a complex or extensive essay. The underlying principle is to provide the reader with a sort of outline of the essay's content.

The Road-Map Introduction

> Thesis (main idea)
> Reference to each major point of the essay
> A concluding sentence that returns, in different words,
>   to the thesis

Here is an example of this type of introduction for an essay on the novels of Charles Dickens:

> Dickens's novels often present children as the adults or "parents" in their families. In early works like *Nicholas Nickleby*, the real parents are basically unreliable.
> The children cannot count on them for support, guidance, or love. But the problem intensifies in works like *Bleak House* where adults often act like children. In Dickens's last completed novel, *Our Mutual Friend*, Jenny Wren and Lizzie Hexam suggest the final extension of this theme: they are mothers to their own fathers. Throughout Dickens's works it is the children who run things and hold the families together, while the adults fantasize, dream, or drink.

This introduction does not actually discuss the examples or prove the point of the essay, but it leaves no doubt as to what will be discussed and in what order. It names the thesis, outlines three supporting points that will be treated (*Nicholas Nickleby, Bleak House,* and *Our Mutual Friend*), and allows the reader to see the general plan of the whole essay. This type of introduction is most common in scientific and social science writing and provides the reader with an "abstract" of the essay.

The General-to-Specific Introduction

The other type of introduction does not outline the paper. Instead, it draws the reader into the topic slowly, leaving the presentation of individual points to the body of the essay:

> A general statement (in the topic area)
> More specific statements that lead to thesis
> Thesis (main idea)

Here is an example of this type of introduction for the same paper on the novels of Dickens:

> The nineteenth century took the family seriously. Queen Victoria and Prince Albert were a model family, the parents of nine children. And in the novels that were meant to be read to the family group, family connections and relationships were major themes. Charles Dickens felt the presence of these themes and, as the unhappily married father of 10 children, knew what family life was like. His novels, however, often present the family in a rather inverted manner.

This introduction slowly defines the areas to be discussed and gradually brings the reader to the topic. The sample begins with the nineteenth century and nineteenth-century families, then goes on to Dickens's own family, and finally to the families in Dickens's novels. The actual novels are not named, but the topic is suggested in the last sentence.

This type of introduction is remarkably flexible. It can be brief or lengthy. The opening can be many things; for example, background information—a few words about the author and the time period—begin this essay. A definition could also have been used. A science paper on eating habits might want to define "eating" in a broader sense than usual in order to discuss ingestive behaviors in one-celled organisms. This type of introduction could also begin with a common assumption and then contradict it:

> Jobs are scarce. Unemployment is up and people are holding on to whatever jobs they have. There's not much movement in major corporations and, when people retire or depart, their work is absorbed by the survivors. Yet this may be the best time in the last 10 years to look for a new job.

Newspapers and magazines like *Time* and *Newsweek* often use this introduction strategy, capturing the reader's attention with a brief story or incident:

> The hot night of July 26, 1999 threatened a thunderstorm in Henderson, Texas. When Nancy-Jean Alberts went out to empty the trash, she noticed the sky was dark for 8 p.m. and lines of heat lightning darted along the horizon.

This article might turn out to be about a murder, a flood, or even trash. The narration at the beginning catches the readers' attention and draws them into the paragraph; a forceful and focused thesis statement will follow.

The general-to-specific introduction is flexible and simple. You have some choices in its construction and do not have to give away all your ideas in the first paragraph. It is suitable for most essays and is especially useful for those in a timed situation when you may not know at the beginning exactly what points (or how many) you will cover. The only pitfall is the first sentence—do not make it overly general. "Life is interesting" doesn't sound very interesting and would require a very lengthy paragraph to narrow it down adequately to a thesis. "Shakespeare is a great playwright" is certainly more specific, but it lacks impact. Don't let the first sentence grab the reader too vigorously, either. An attention-getter is a good idea but it can be overused or overdone. Remember your audience and let it dictate your tone. You don't want to begin:

> Wha-a-a-a-a! Who's that howling in *Bleak House*? Is it a crying baby or is it simply Mr. Skimpole?

Make the first sentence interesting and related to the thesis but try to engage the reader's interest without being confusing or shocking.

Is an Introduction Absolutely Necessary?

Most essays need a paragraph of some length to identify the topic and get things going, but there are a few exceptions. A short essay (one or two paragraphs) does not need an introduction. A few sentences at the beginning of the first paragraph can make the topic clear. Some tests and examinations (and some college application essays) provide only a few minutes or a few inches for your responses. In such a case, a full introduction would waste precious time and space. If you are given an essay test with several questions, do not fret over the introduction for a *15-point* question, "To what extent did Metternich influence diplomacy in the nineteenth century?" Begin with one or two sentences drawn from the question itself (you might simply state that Metternich *did* change diplomatic techniques) and give the rest of the allotted time and space to the *proof.*

Another time to consider omitting the introduction is in an inductive essay. This essay takes the reader through a discussion without a clear focus, revealing its intention only at the end. This is a suspenseful and creative approach to the essay and can be very effective. But, it is best reserved for less stressful situations than the college essay, for the most able writers, and for short, creative topics.

Finally, a narrative essay might survive without an introduction. The writer tells a story, recounts a series of incidents, and then draws meaning from them in the conclusion. Like the inductive essay, this format requires readers to go some distance on faith. They aren't sure to what they ought to be paying attention, but finally, it all makes sense in the conclusion. This strategy can make a very effective *short* college essay, but remember, it puts a significant burden on the reader and is best reserved for occasional use.

Most of the time, you'll want an introduction and most often either the road-map or the general-to-specific format will give your essay a strong start and a clear direction.

The Body

The substance of your essay is the body. Bound in place by the introduction and the conclusion, the body does the work of the essay: It proves. It presents the evidence that will convert the reader to your opinion. Each paragraph of the body is a block of proof, a chunk of evidence of the validity of your claim, and each is developed from one aspect or point of your thesis, as sketched out in the simple outline.

The Shakespeare essay, for example, uses three plays as examples to prove that Shakespeare was concerned with the restoration of order. The outline gives three subtopics: order in *Romeo and Juliet*, in *The Taming of the Shrew,* and in *Hamlet.* Thus, you plan three paragraphs for the body, one for each play. If, however, in drafting the essay you discover new aspects of the topic that should be mentioned—perhaps that *Hamlet* is a play about both the proper order in a kingdom and also about one man's drive for personal order and revenge for the death of his father—the plan can be expanded and the number of paragraphs in the body adjusted, in this case, to four, one for each play and two for *Hamlet.*

The important thing is to prove, with specific and vivid detail, the correctness of your claim. You must present a sequence of *arguments* for your thesis rather than plot summaries, story outlines, or a review of the course of history thus far.

Selection is the key. You must go through each part of your argument and select the scenes, details, quotations, and facts that show the truth of your view. To substantiate your thesis, you *must* bring to the reader's attention only that evidence that cumulatively shows that you are correct. Select. Do not retell! It is not persuasive to retell a whole story, review every event a war, or summarize everything that has been said on your topic. Your essay should be based on your angle of vision, your special lens, your way of looking at a larger complex of ideas. And in support of your thesis, you need to gather *only* those points or ideas that prove your view is right.

Each paragraph of the body should conform to this pattern (or vary from it for a *good* reason):

Topic Sentence
(the main idea of this paragraph and its relation to the thesis)
Development
(the evidence—events, facts, statistics, reasons, examples,
details, things said in the literature, things said about the
literature—presented in some logical order)
End Sentence
(especially useful in a long or complex paragraph)

Topic Sentences

The topic sentence is important in two ways: It identifies the subject of
the paragraph, and it shows how the paragraph is connected to the
thesis. It may even form a transition from the previous paragraph.

1. thesis — Shakespeare explored the instability of life and the
2. transition — need for order not only in a comic setting but also
3. topic — in the tragic circumstances of Prince Hamlet.

1. topic — But things get worse in *Our Mutual Friend.*
2. transition — Now parents and adults are not just silly and
3. thesis — irresponsible; they are the children of the families.

In the first example, the writer reiterates, in slightly different words,
the main thesis of the essay, mentions the point of the previous paragraph (a comedy's treatment of this theme), and then establishes what
this paragraph will discuss (*Hamlet*). In the second instance, the writer
uses two sentences to get going: the first names the paragraph's topic
(*Our Mutual Friend*); the second fits that topic into the larger scheme
of the thesis (irresponsibility and childish adults).

There is, and always should be, flexibility in a format. Every paragraph does not have to begin with a reference to the preceding paragraph. A topic sentence doesn't have to be first in a paragraph, either.
But each sentence that appears before the topic sentence runs the risk
of being wasted. Your readers don't yet know what's going on and may
lose interest or the sense of continuity. They ask, "Why am I reading
this?" Therefore, it is helpful if each paragraph declares—and usually
the sooner the better—its topic and how it intends to support it.

Development

The middle of each paragraph is the support. It is a combination of facts, events, quotations, examples, and reasons that proves the point of that paragraph and, in so doing, proves the thesis of the essay. It is the evidence that will persuade your reader. Notice the combination of different types of support in this paragraph from an essay about insanity in *Moby Dick*.

Another way Melville makes the reader aware of the transition from sanity to insanity is in his imagery. Throughout the novel, he weaves a careful pattern of images that turn from normal to abnormal, from familiar to strange. For example, the images of fire begin in the — Example friendly inns of Nantucket and New Bedford. Ishmael rejoices in the privilege of "making my own summer — Quotation with my own coals" (61). Fire is here warmth and companionship. Even Queequeg's sacrificial fire to Yojo — Event serves as the beginning of intimate friendship between the two sailors. But slowly this begins to change. By the middle of the novel, fire begins to suggest evil. It is associated with Ahab's mad purpose, what critic — Critic's Richard Chase in *The American Novel and Its Tradition* — Opinion calls "the self-absorption that leads to isolation, madness and suicide" (109). Ahab calls himself a volcano in "The Quarter-Deck" chapter and the crew — Event swears death to Moby Dick in a fiery crossing of harpoons. Later, in the chapter called "The Tryworks," — Detail Ishmael compares the rendering fires to the fires of hell. — Event By Chapter 113, hot-forged harpoons are being dipped in blood as Ahab baptizes the crew "*in nomine* — Quotation *diabolis*" (373). Nature's fire, lightning, warns the crew — Events away by igniting the masts and nearly striking Ahab. The happy homefires of Nantucket have changed into the dangerous fires of Ahab's mad passion; thus they reinforce the novel's movement from sanity to insanity.

Like Melville's imagery, his characters, too, move toward madness. First there is Pip . . . .

End Sentence

At the end of a paragraph, a sentence that summarizes the whole paragraph and refocuses on the essay's thesis can strengthen the essay's coherence. Because this sentence echoes the topic sentence, a student may wonder if the paper isn't getting repetitious. "Isn't it awfully boring to say this one thing at the beginning and end of the paper, and at the beginning and end of every paragraph, too?" Remember, however, that you are covering ideas familiar and clear only to you. You must make them equally clear to readers who have never thought exactly this way about this topic. They have to be led a little. There has to be repetition. Each topic sentence should sound somewhat alike. Each should relate to the thesis. The concluding sentences of some, or all, of the body paragraphs will return to the main idea of the essay, too. There will be changes in wording and perhaps only the repetition of a key word (such as "order" in the Shakespeare essay) to remind readers of what's happening. But don't think you're helping them by retelling the plot. Provide signs, repetitions, along the way to keep readers on *your path*. The end of the paragraph about *Moby Dick* is a good example of this kind of helpful repetition.

A short or simple paragraph, or one that appears right before the conclusion, does not need the summary sentence at the end. You can draw the paragraph to a close in some other way, perhaps simply by adding a sentence that makes it clear the paragraph is complete.

Remember to follow a logical order in the presentation of the body's paragraphs. Chronological order or order of location are possible types of organization. Another excellent choice is order of importance, beginning with your minor points and building toward your most important argument at the end.

The body of the essay is its most important part. You marshal all the evidence you can find to support your theory and present it in a series of paragraphs designed to convince your readers. Most of these paragraphs will begin with a topic sentence that connects the paragraph to the thesis. All of them will be made up of facts, examples, and extensive specific support for your claim. Many will end with the summarizing clincher that redirects the reader's attention to the thesis. The repetitions of the thesis and its rewording in topic sentences and end sentences aren't useless reiterations; they are the necessary coherence that creates the focus. The body should be by far the greatest percentage of the essay for it is there that the essay will win its argument.

Points to Remember

Patterns are useful. Good tailors begin with standard patterns and soon develop their own. So it is with writers. The idea is to begin with rules and use them where appropriate. There is no reason why you can't "break" a rule as long as you have a reason and are doing so consciously. The goal of any writing advice is to help writers be more aware and in control of their material and to avoid writing with no idea of what they should do or why they are at one point succeeding and at another failing. More than any student comment, "You didn't like my paper" is the one that drives me crazy. I have never graded a paper on whether I liked it or not. I have always determined a grade according to how successful the student was in organizing the material and in validating his or her argument. The paper made its own grade.

Also, keep in mind that there is no secret set of "right" answers stashed in the school safe. The purpose of an essay is not to guess what the teacher believes about a topic and win an A; it is to develop a good thesis and prove it. Critical opinion changes, even among the leaders in a given field. Notice the ups and downs that the reputations of presidents suffer. Consider the esteem with which Freud was regarded in the 1950s versus the respect awarded him in the feminist age. To paraphrase Emerson, "Ask for no man's opinion but your own." Every age must write its own criticism. So the essay is not about latching onto THE ONE RIGHT ANSWER. It is about your ability to find a possible answer and to make a convincing argument for it.

This is especially true for the college essay. Many students set out to "tell them what they want to hear." This is a fruitless and contradictory goal. What the essay should provide is a sense of you, a concrete and specific view with the facts to back it up.

An interesting idea with no evidence is a pointless exercise in creativity; a lot of plot review or a collection of facts without a focus is merely exposition. Think of two opposing lawyers; each has the same events and facts to work with yet the prosecutor selects and presents them so the accused looks like a cold-blooded murderer while the attorney for the defense selects and presents them so that the client seems as innocent as an angel. Every essay needs a good thesis and a focused selection of supporting material to make it clear and convincing.

Do not wander off this straight and narrow path to either side: to the "let's-tell-'em-what-they-want-to-hear" essay that presents a razzle-dazzle idea with no evidence, or to the "let's-tell-'em-all-we-know-and-hope-for-the-best" (travelog/autobiography) essay that is full of facts with no focus. In any essay (and especially in the college essay), you need both *focus* and *proof.*

A Special Organizational Problem

The Comparative Essay

The comparative essay is a special assignment. It is a challenging format that is often used for Advanced Placement Program Exam questions and final examination topics. The organization is not difficult as long as you keep in mind the comparative purpose of the paper. The pitfall is writing a comparative essay that never does any comparing—lots of information with no comparisons drawn between the points. A history student, for example, asked to compare the programs set up to regulate business that were passed in the administration of Woodrow Wilson with those passed in the administration of Franklin D. Roosevelt, might recount all she knows about Wilson, then all she knows about Roosevelt, and then conclude. This is not a comparison.

One way to get it right is to discuss the first item of the comparison, in this case Wilson's regulatory programs, then discuss the second item in the same order used in the previous paragraph and with *constant reference* to what has *already* been said about Wilson. The second paragraph will include sentences such as the following:

> Roosevelt had opposition similar to that confronted by Wilson, but he employed different tactics to overcome it.

> But like Wilson, Roosevelt found his backers were fickle.

> These measures finally were more successful than what Wilson accomplished.

Proceed in sequence through your points, sticking with the order established in the first paragraph of the body, continually making comparative comments about the similarities and differences of each new point to what has already been discussed. The conclusion for this essay should summarize fully and methodically all the comparisons that you have discussed in the essay.

Another—better—method of organization, more likely to be used in an essay prepared outside of class than for an examination question, separates aspects of the comparison. In the example below, the writer isolates individual aspects of the topic—creation of programs, implementation, obstacles, success, impact—and then looked at each president's handling of them. Here is a pair of outlines that shows the difference between the two ways of writing a comparison:

A. *Comparing Wilson and FDR*
1. Wilson
   a. programs
   b. implementation
   c. obstacles
   d. success
   e. impact
2. FDR (with reference to Wilson)
   a. programs
   b. implementation
   c. obstacles
   d. success
   e. impact
3. Comparative summary

B. *Comparing Wilson and FDR*
1. Creation of programs
   a. Wilson
   b. FDR
2. Implementation
   a. Wilson
   b. FDR
3. Obstacles
   a. Wilson
   b. FDR
4. Success
   a. Wilson
   b. FDR
5. Long-term impact
   a. Wilson
   b. FDR
6. Short conclusion
   a. Wilson
   b. FDR

The second way does not necessarily cover more material than the first, but it is more directly comparative and more clearly organized. The reader can follow the comparisons easily, and the conclusion doesn't have to do as much. Like a lot of things in life, the second way is harder...but better!

The Conclusion

The conclusion can serve one or two functions. It should refocus the readers' attention on the main idea of the essay, remind them of what they have just read, and reaffirm the validity of the author's argument. This is the summary conclusion and, although not particularly creative, it gets the job done. The format is:

> Thesis (slightly reworded)
> Reference to the major points of the body (in order)
> End sentence

A more creative use of the conclusion is as a springboard for a new idea. After refocusing and briefly summarizing, the writer goes on to judge, speculate, generalize, or recommend.

> Thesis (slightly reworded)
> Short summary of the essay
> Additional idea that grows logically from what
>   has been proven in the essay

This type of conclusion does not suit every topic, as there will be times when you do not have anything to add to the end of your essay. But, there are many times when it can work for you. Here are four examples:

1. The essay on Shakespeare's theme of order might end with a generalization about Elizabethan England and the order that people in that time saw throughout their world. You would thus connect this particular theme from three of Shakespeare's plays to larger trends and ideas of his age.
2. An essay on the athletic facilities at your school, in which you urge the creation of an all-weather track, might recommend the creation of a capital fund campaign to raise the money needed for the project. The essay itself would only show the need and value of the track. Having reiterated those ideas in the conclusion, you could go on to suggest how the work might get done.
3. An essay on a gerbil experiment might speculate on other possible parallel experiments that could be performed.
4. A college essay describing an applicant might use the conclusion to connect goals and personal qualities to the college itself. For example, if

you have proven you are a science buff, in your conclusion you might show why MIT is the logical choice for you.

To determine whether this type of conclusion is appropriate, at the end of your essay ask yourself, "So what? What does all that I've proven mean? Where can I go from here?" If there isn't any real answer to this, then sum up and stop. But if a suggestion or generalization comes to mind, you might use it for a springboard conclusion. This conclusion is especially useful for assigned essay topics that request the writer to discuss two unequal ideas. For example, a history teacher might ask: "To what extent did the role of women in society change during the 1930s? Do you see any parallels in the situation of women today?" The real heart of this question is the role of women in the 1930s. An additional, although less important, part of the question asks the student to assess his or her life in terms of what's been said about the 1930s. The student constructs an essay with individual paragraphs devoted to areas of change concerning women: the domestic scene, the job market, economic power, fashion. The conclusion might sum up these points and then go on to comment on the writer's own time. Since this is a lesser part of the question, it could be adequately treated as the final aspect of a conclusion. Judgments and comparisons could be based on what has already been said in the body.

This second type of conclusion would not be a good choice if the question asked for the discussion of two *equal* points: "Discuss the forces that created the League of Nations and those that destroyed it." Here, the best bet is a body divided into two sections, one on creation and one on destruction. The conclusion would then merely summarize what was presented in the body.

As you plan and write the essay, how much you say, the importance of the various parts of the essay, the structure of the paragraphs themselves, and the repetition needed will emerge. You will choose an introduction that suits your topic, create body paragraphs in support of your thesis, and select an appropriate conclusion.

Transition

Fifty years ago, on an early nature program called *Wild Kingdom*, the host always tried to create a strong transition between the show and the commercials:

> That lion cub was almost eaten by those jackals. But luckily his father was there to protect him. You'll feel that same security when you're protected by (sponsor's name) insurance.

By repeating a key word (such as protect) and using demonstratives (that, those) and transitional expressions (but), the host established a connection between the program and the advertisements.

Transition is still the most important stylistic skill you can master. It is the way to create connections and coherence in your writing. It is absolutely essential to a smooth introduction, important within and especially at the beginning of body paragraphs, and helpful as you move into the conclusion.

There are three major ways to create transition:

Rule 1

Use transitional expressions. These words and phrases make connections wherever they appear:

To show time or sequence: first, second, then
To show cause: therefore, thus, hence
To show similarity: and, like, similarly, likewise
To show difference: on the other hand, however

Example: Ahab sees Moby Dick as his goal in life. *Likewise,* Jay Gatsby sees Daisy as his goal.

Rule 2

Repeat key words and sentence structure (parallelism).

Example: Ahab *sees* Moby Dick as *his goal* in life. Likewise, Jay Gatsby *sees* Daisy *as his goal.* (Note the repetition of the words "sees" and "goal" and the use of parallel sentence structure.)

Example: "...that government of the *people,* by the *people,* for the *people,* shall not perish from the earth." ("People" is repeated in a series of three prepositional phrases.)

Rule 3

Use pronouns (he, she, it, they) and demonstrative nouns and adjectives (this, that).

Example: Francis Bacon: He that hath wife and children hath given
hostages to fortune, for *they* are impediments to great enterprise…."

Example: Franklin D. Roosevelt: "The New Deal is our hope.
It is the way to recovery. *It* is the immediate way. *It* is the strongest
assurance that the recovery will endure."

The following paragraph relies heavily on transition to guide the reader.
Notice the different methods used, particularly the paragraph hooks.

Another way Melville makes the reader aware of the transition from sanity to insanity is in his imagery. Throughout the novel, he weaves a careful pattern of images that turn from normal to abnormal, from familiar to strange. For example, the images of fire begin in the friendly inns of Nantucket and New Bedford. Ishmael rejoices in the privilege of "making my own summer with my own coals" (61). Fire is here warmth and companionship. Even Queequeg's sacrificial fire to Yojo serves as the beginning of intimate friendship between the two sailors. But slowly this begins to change. By the middle of the novel, fire begins to suggest evil. It is associated with Ahab's mad purpose, what critic Richard Chase in *The American Novel and Its Tradition* calls "the self-absorption that leads to isolation, madness and suicide" (109). Ahab calls himself a volcano in "The Quarter-Deck" chapter and the crew swears death to Moby Dick in a fiery crossing of harpoons. Later, in the chapter called "The Tryworks," Ishmael compares the rendering fires to the fires of hell. By Chapter 113, hot-forged harpoons are being dipped in blood as Ahab baptizes the crew *"in nomine diabolis"* (373). Nature's fire, lightning, warns the crew away by igniting the masts and nearly striking Ahab. The happy homefires of Nantucket have changed into the dangerous fires of Ahab's mad passion; thus they reinforce the novel's movement from sanity to insanity.

Like Melville's imagery, his characters too move toward madness. First there is Pip . . . .

Word Repetition

Pronouns and Demonstrative Adjective

Transitional Expressions

Paragraph Hook

Try to keep transition in mind as you draft and especially as you revise your essay. It will provide the flow and cohesiveness that every essay needs.

Editing

The final stage of the essay process is editing. Proofread your essay carefully and slowly; read it aloud. Look for:

FOCUS: Check for coherence throughout the essay so that the reader can find the main idea (thesis) and follow it from beginning to end. You might have someone read your introduction to see what he or she thinks your essay is about. If there's any doubt in the reader's mind, keep rewriting that paragraph. Also be sure your main idea is not only clear in your introduction but is referred to *throughout* the essay, especially at the beginning of body paragraphs.

PROOF: Be sure the development of each body paragraph is extensive, specific, and clearly related to your main point. This is the meat of the sandwich—make it substantial.

CORRECTNESS: Check your spelling (or use a spelling checker on your computer). Even for some very bright people, spelling is a problem. Find a good dictionary and check every word you're unsure of. Don't be lazy about spelling. I know a recruiter who turned down a good job candidate because he hadn't bothered to spell the company name properly in his application letter. "He's careless; he'll only cause headaches for me and hassles and embarrassment at the top." Right or wrong, we are often judged on small things.

In a second reading, try to pay attention to *how* things are said, in addition to what you have said. Try to read with the eyes of an enemy looking for problems, keeping the following in mind:

1. A simple style is best. Good writing sounds like speech rather than a vocabulary review lesson. Where you are having problems expressing an idea, try using shorter sentences and simpler words rather than longer sentences and a thesaurus.

2. Evaluate your writing for sentence variety. Write some long, complex sentences; use a short sentence once in a while for impact. Don't begin all your sentences with the subject or with the same word.

3. Remember your audience and the requirements of the assignment. There are differences in the structure, style, and precision required in a science journal and in a finished lab report, in an essay for your drama class and in a final term paper in a Shakespeare seminar for senior English majors.

4. As in everything, there are usage conventions and somewhat arbitrary rules of formality. Most academic writing requires that you observe these conventions, although each audience will be a little different and each teacher may have his or her own pet peeves. Usually these are explained early in a course or described in the writing handbook recommended by the teacher. In general:

   - Avoid dashes and exclamation points. They are the junk food of the punctuation world, just as the semicolon is the truffle. The former are too casual for the tone of most essays; the latter is best used sparingly.
   - Avoid parentheses. Most often the sentence merely needs reorganization.
   - Avoid asking a lot of questions. An essay should answer questions. Asking them is contrived, because you intend to answer them yourself.
   - Avoid setting off expressions that are wrong to begin with in sanitizing quotation marks. "Monet was really 'into' water lilies" is a mismatch of style and substance. Don't try to get away with it by putting "into" in quotation marks. Choose a different word: "Monet found water lilies fascinating."
   - Avoid contractions, abbreviations, and slang. Keep your style reasonably formal and scrupulously correct.

Set the essay aside for a few days—unless it's due tomorrow! If it is, take this moment to resolve not to wait until the last minute next time.

When you think you are ready to look at your essay with a fresh, objective eye, go back, reread it, and make any changes that will improve the final draft. Once you are satisfied, it is time for a little outside evaluation. Ask someone whose writing ability you respect to read your essay. The writing center at your school is a good option. Try to pick a reader whose comments aren't threatening to you so you can really hear what he or she is saying. Your boyfriend or girlfriend is probably not the best choice.

Ultimately, you are the best editor. No one can speak for you; your own words and ideas are your best bet. Be sure to proofread the final draft several times yourself to eliminate unnecessary words and all errors in spelling, punctuation, and grammar. Errors are distracting and undermine the points you are making, so proofread, proofread, proofread! Spell-checking programs aren't enough.

Understanding and Avoiding Plagiarism

You've heard the word *plagiarism* but may not know precisely what it means. Taking someone else's words or ideas and presenting them as your own is a form of stealing called plagiarism. Quotations from *Hamlet* in a paper on *Hamlet* are the support for your theory. Words and ideas from critics who agree with you add credibility to your argument, whether you quote them directly or paraphrase their words. But you must always give credit where credit is due. Identify in the text or by footnotes all direct quotations, paraphrases, and borrowed ideas. It doesn't matter whether the source is today's newspaper, an out-of-print book, or a friend's research report; you must acknowledge the use of *any* borrowed material. For complete rules on how to cite borrowed material, consult your English class handbook or the *MLA Handbook for Writers of Research Papers* (see the bibliography at the end of this book).

Reviewing the Process

The Essay: The written defense of a claim
    Two Options for Introductions:
    The Road-Map Introduction
        Thesis
        Major Points
        End Sentence
    The General-to-Specific Introduction
        A General Statement in the Topic Area
        Increasingly Specific Statements
        Thesis

The Body: Present a series of ideas to support your claim
    A Sample Body Paragraph
        Topic Sentence (states topic of paragraph, shows relation of
            paragraph to thesis, may show transition from the previous
            paragraph)
        Development (extensive specific examples and evidence to
            support your point …about 80 percent of the paragraph)
        End Sentence

Two Options for Conclusions:
    Summary Conclusion
        Thesis
        Major Points
        End Sentence
    Speculative Conclusion
        Thesis
        Short Summary of Essay
        New but Related Point (generalization, speculation, judgment,
            recommendation)

The essay process begins with the gathering of ideas by brainstorming, a process that should result in a specific thesis and a simple outline. This can take three minutes during a final examination or several weeks in the preparation of a research paper. Depending on the length and complexity of the topic, you may or may not want to refine and expand the simple outline as you continue to plan, research, and prepare.

Once you're writing, create an introduction that makes your thesis clear. (The introduction can also make your whole essay plan clear.) The body is the proof and should be a careful selection of points that validate your thesis. A conclusion at the end should sum up what you've said or raise further possibilities.

Keep your style simple and stress transition between ideas and between paragraphs.

Edit your work yourself and with some outside help. You will probably want to consult a writing handbook for the fine points of style, grammar, research, and footnoting. Check the Suggested Reading list in the back of this book for the names of some helpful reference books. Make a final copy of your essay, proofread it three times, and feel satisfied at having followed a process through from beginning to end.

The essay is a marvelously flexible form. Its only strict requirements are a clear and continual focus and plenty of proof. "Tell 'em what you're gonna tell 'em, tell 'em, tell 'em what you told 'em." Use a beginning to present your thesis, a middle full of persuasive evidence, and an end that returns to and reaffirms the thesis.

Remember that the advice in this chapter is not intended to be an inflexible set of dos and don'ts for writing. These are suggestions, beginnings; some you will always use, some you will outgrow. All are designed to put you in control of your own writing.

Chapter 4
Writing an Application Essay

> Two roads diverged in a yellow wood,
> And sorry I could not travel both
> And be one traveler, long I stood
> And looked down one as far as I could
> To where it bent in the undergrowth;
> Then took the other, as just as fair . . . .
>
> *from "The Road Not Taken" by Robert Frost*

We define ourselves by our choices. The big ones shape our lives: what path to take, what career, who to marry, where to live. But even small choices are self-defining: Do you prefer the top half of the bagel or the bottom? Pepsi or herbal tea? J. D. Salinger or Stephen King? Mac or PC? Colleges believe that by observing the process of choosing, they gain insight into the applicant. Thus, most application essays are experiments in choice. *How* you write the essay will reveal your writing abilities. *What* you write about will reveal you.

Here is a sampling of the application essay questions from a wide variety of colleges and universities—small, private, and selective institutions and large state colleges. Remember, the small and selective colleges often maintain a more personal admissions process and may require more than one essay. They rate the essay as a major piece in the puzzle. But even large colleges and universities such as Brigham Young, Boston University, and Pace University suggest or require an essay, and turn to it for additional insight in special situations, or to settle "gray zone" applications.

Colleges and Their Questions

"If you could balance on a tightrope, over what landscape would you walk? (No net)." (University of Chicago)

"If you are applying to the Pratt School of Engineering, please discuss why you want to study engineering and why you would like to study at Duke." (Duke University)

"Indicate a person who has had a significant influence on you, and describe that influence." (The Common Application)

Amherst College offers five quotations and asks for your response. This quotation is one of the options: "Memory: Is there a more fragile human faculty? Without it, what are we? It is the only record we have of who we were and what we want to become. Take it away and only a spiritless machine is left, free of conviction, free of purpose." —Ilan Stavans

Many applications ask questions that need more than one-word answers but are not actually essays. As you look over your applications, begin by making a list of all the questions you have to answer. There will be a duplication of questions and you may be able to recycle some of your answers with minimal changes. Schools that accept the Common Application (there are over 240) make life a little easier. And various wordings of the question "Describe yourself" or "Write an essay that gives a sense of you as an individual" appear on many applications.

Don't, however, plan to use the same answer for two entirely different questions. Carol Lunkenheimer, at Northwestern, warns: "We can recognize Stanford's or Dartmouth's question. We want an applicant who cares enough about Northwestern to write an original essay for *our* application." And don't use your answer to "What interests you about Loyola College?" for "What specific aspect of Barnard College would you be most excited to experience if admitted?" There will probably be some similarities in course offerings, programs, location, or philosophy among the colleges you apply to, but the "Why us?" questions need answers tailored to each individual school.

Once you've sketched out what you have to do, you can see that your answers will vary in length. Some questions provide an inch or two for the answer; some give a full page with the offer of additional sheets if needed. Stick as closely as possible to the space provided. The college is suggesting how extensive and complex an answer they want by how much paper they supply. Let that be your guideline. Don't fall too short or go much beyond the limit. Readers are assigned many folders to evaluate and are not perusing your application at their leisure. Make your answers *very legible* and to the point. In all likelihood, three or four pages in a cramped, bunched-up scribble will be skimmed; you'll get more attention with a concise, typed piece.

Short-Answer Questions

The real difference among the questions is the issue of choice. Some questions ask for a simple list of activities, summer work, jobs, honors, or recent reading. These questions are not difficult and do not require soul-searching. Some schools even ask for this information in the form of a chart. The simple résumé you created for your guidance counselor or your recommending teacher will help with these descriptive questions.

As a List

List the items chronologically from most recent to most remote, or from most important to least. Provide complete information and follow the same format for each item:

June–August 2004   Lifeguard
                          Springfield Town Pool
                          40 hours per week
                          $7.00 per hour

June–August 2003   Swimming instructor
                          Springfield Day Camp
                          20 hours per week
                          $8.00 per hour

In Paragraph Form

Include the activity, your involvement, and the time commitment. Be sure to clarify names of groups or titles; *The Mirror* or Key Club by themselves are not clear to admissions personnel. As one admissions staffer put it, "At some schools the Spanish Club is just a bunch of kids who get together on Friday nights for tacos." Make it clear that your activities have involved responsibility and effort.

1. I am president of the Book Worms, a school club that does volunteer work for the town library. Each month I attend one two-hour planning meeting with the library staff and schedule time slots and assignments for the 11 other club members; I work at the reference desk from 7 to 9 p.m. every Tuesday night.
2. During my junior year, I was assistant sports editor for *The Mirror,* our monthly school newspaper. I wrote at least one story for each monthly issue and edited one or two articles by the junior high sportswriter for each issue.

Don't list minor involvements, jobs you held for a week, or a book you meant to read but didn't. A list of impressive activities that you know nothing about and have done nothing more than sign up for is worthless and dishonest. The student who founded the Animal Rights Club in May of his junior year and now lists himself as president is clearly not so much interested in animal rights as in nice-looking credentials on his application. And the less said the better about the girl who listed her favorite book as *Canterberry [sic] Tales.* These questions ask for simple, matter-of-fact answers about what has interested you and engaged your time; be complete, clear, and—above all—honest.

The Real Essays

If the application asks you to select *one* activity, achievement, or experience and discuss what it means to you, the question requires a response, whether short or long, that is not simply factual—it requires choice. These are the tough ones. They come in three varieties:

The "You" Question

Most of these boil down to "tell us about yourself." Some examples:

1. A personal statement

> "Write an essay which conveys to the reader a sense of who you are." (Columbia University)
>
> "Complete a one-page personal statement. You can use the personal statement to highlight special interests, talents, goals, or unique experiences." (James Madison University)
>
> "Who are you? Eugene Lang College acknowledges the unique characteristics of its applicants.... Provide us with a creative definition of yourself." (Eugene Lang College)

2. Describe a significant experience, interest, challenge, or value.

> "Describe an achievement, significant experience, or challenge that you feel has been important in strengthening your personal values." (Bentley College)
>
> "Recall an occasion when you took a risk that you now know was the right thing to do." (University of Pennsylvania)
>
> "Evaluate a significant experience, achievement, risk you have taken, or ethical dilemma you have faced and its impact on you." (Common Application)

3. How have you grown and developed?

> "Describe a situation in which you have made a difference in your school or community and what you learned from that experience." (Gettysburg College)
>
> "Explain a time when you experienced or learned a custom that was new to you." (Juniata College)
>
> "In the space provided below or on a separate sheet if necessary, please describe which of these activities ... has had the most meaning for you and why." (Common Application)

The "Why Us?" Question

These questions focus on your choice of school or career as self-reflective. Some examples:

4. Why have you selected College X?

> "What do you think you would gain from the educational experience at Bryn Mawr and what would you contribute to the community?" (Bryn Mawr College)

> "Please compose an essay about yourself that tells us how you will help the university to carry out its mission." (University of San Francisco)

> "What are the qualities and characteristics of Davidson that appeal to you, and what contributions do you anticipate making as a Davidson student?" (Davidson College)

5. Why have you chosen this program or profession?

> "We would like to know, in no more than 500 words, what experiences have led you to select your professional field and objective." (Boston University)

> "On what kind of projects do you enjoy working? What kind of problems do you enjoy solving? What area of engineering interests you most?" (Johns Hopkins University, engineering programs)

> "Please submit a one-page essay that explains why you have chosen your major, department, or program. This essay should include the reasons why you've chosen the major, any goals or relevant work plans, and any other information you would like us to know." (Carnegie Mellon University)

The Creative Question

6. The issue question

> "Briefly discuss a current global issue, indicating why you consider it important and what you suggest should be done to deal with it." (Georgetown University)

"Our world has seen some major advancements in technology over the past 10 to 15 years. Is this a good thing?" (Lehigh University)

7. The hero or influential person question

"What character or characters from fiction, film, theater, or television intrigued you or taught you something and why?" (Barnard College)

"Indicate a person who has had a significant influence on you, and describe that influence." (Common Application)

The Cultural Work/Fiction Question

"If you could recommend one work of fiction to your UNC classmates, what would you ask them to read and contemplate?" (University of North Carolina)

"What cultural work (a specific work of literature, art, dance, music, or science) has had a significant impact on your life?" (Spelman College)

9. A quotation to comment on

"In his autobiography *A Long Walk to Freedom*, Nelson Mandela writes, 'There is nothing like returning to a place that remains unchanged to find the ways in which you yourself have altered.' Tell us about an unchanging place to which you have returned ... How does its constancy reveal changes in you?" (University of Chicago)

"French Enlightenment philosopher Denis Diderot once wrote: 'The aim of an encyclopedia is to collect all knowledge scattered over the face of the earth, to present its general outlines and structure to the [people] with whom we live, and to transmit this to those who will come after us, so that the work of past centuries may be useful to future centuries, that our children, by becoming more educated, may at the same time become more virtuous and happier....' What values and attitudes does Diderot reveal? What are his assumptions? Do you

SPANISH CLUB
MEETING TO NIGHT

SPECIAL TOPIC:
JALAPENOS AND YOU

agree with his analysis of the benefits of education?"
(Trinity College, Washington, D.C.)

10. Imagining the future

"What are your personal goals and professional plans upon
completion of college?" (Loyola College)

"You have just completed your 300-page autobiography. Please
submit page 217." (University of Pennsylvania)

11. An academic essay or school paper

"Please submit an original graded paper." (Simmons College)

"Please attach a 2–5 page analytical essay written for one of your
classes in the eleventh or twelfth grade. The paper must include
your teacher's comments and your grade." (Vassar College)

"Please submit a copy of a research, expository, or creative paper
(in the English language) with instructor comments." (Reed
College)

12. Others

"Step out your front door and tell us what you would change
about what you see." (Lehigh University)

"Discuss the importance of creativity as a means of expression and the influences that have been most important in your own creative endeavors. To supplement your written essay, you may also provide examples of your work."
(Earlham College)

"Design an experiment that attempts to determine whether toads can hear. Provide the rationale for your design—explain your reasons for setting up the experiment as you did. Strive for simplicity and clarity.... There are many imaginative ways to approach this problem; you do not need to be a scientist or to do any special research in order to respond well."
(Bennington College)

"Please list three subjects of interest that you have not had the chance to study. Choose one of these, and in a paragraph or two explain what piques your curiosity about this subject and how you would attempt to learn more about it."
(Bard College)

"If at the end of your four years at Pitzer we were to recognize you by citing your contributions to the Pitzer community, what do you think we might say about how you made a difference here?" (Pitzer College)

Underlying all these questions is choice. The question may be direct and ask you to choose something about yourself to discuss, or it may be indirect and require you to write about something either relevant or tangential to the admissions process. Some schools ask you to explain why you chose them or why you chose college at all. Others like a less relevant go-between: choose an event, person, book, quotation, woman of the year, photograph, or invention. You may have to choose a topic; you will certainly have to choose and limit what you include in your response.

Why is the process of choice a significant source of information about the applicant? Why do so many colleges believe they will learn about you—and some think they can learn the most about you—by observing the choices you make? (Note that interviewers employ this technique, too: "If you were a color, what color would you be?" "Whom do you admire most?") First, choosing shows *preferences*. Personality assessments and tests like the Myers-Briggs Type Indicator use preferences to draw conclusions about character, personality, and counseling. Are you an arts person or a hard-facts science type? Certainly, there is a difference between the person who would like to talk to Machiavelli about the cold war and someone who would share a tuna-fish sandwich with Audrey Hepburn to find out what it was like to be a glamorous movie star. The choice would be revealing.

Second, choice also reflects *values*. The person who drives a tomato red Honda Civic until rust leaves nothing for the floorboards to cling to is making a statement about how he wants to spend his money and what he cares about. We say, "That dress isn't me" or "I'm not a cat person." In choosing, you indicate what matters to you and how you perceive yourself.

Third, choosing shows *how* you think. Are you whimsical, a person who chooses on impulse? Or are you methodical, careful, a person who gathers background information before choosing? Questions about you and about career and college reflect these choosing patterns, and even a question about a national issue can show your particular *thinking style, level of intelligence,* and *insight.* The process, too, is under scrutiny here—how carefully the question was considered, how extensively you know the topic, how seriously you regarded the choice.

Do you analyze and think about things that happen to you? Do you feel most comfortable discussing recognized issues, writing about AIDS, South Africa, war in the Middle East? Are you a risk taker, writing an essay that makes a case for itself out of missing socks, lunch with A. A. Milne, the heroic qualities of Jim Henson? Do you respond with a direct answer or get wordy and pompous: "One concept that I've been concerned with recently is reality."

The college regards your choices as a way to evaluate your preferences, values, mental processes, creativity, sense of humor, and depth of knowledge. The writing itself reflects your power of persuasion, organizational abilities, style, and mastery of standard written English. You can see why so many colleges want an essay and why admissions personnel read folder after folder. It's a very fruitful piece of the puzzle. Ten aspects in 500 words! The essay is worth your serious attention. Give it all you've got. IT MATTERS!

The Questions

The goal of all three types of questions is the same: to gather more, and more personal, pieces of the jigsaw puzzle of you for the admissions office to consider. Since the goal is the same—to get you to reveal yourself through your choice—the strategy is the same for handling what seems like, but is not, an incredible diversity of questions.

A Closer Look at the "You" Question

Many colleges ask for an essay specifically about you.

"In what ways have you grown intellectually during your years in high school?"

"Evaluate a significant experience or achievement that has special meaning for you."

"You are strongly encouraged to use the space provided below to describe yourself, your previous academic performance, and your general interests."

"There are limitations to what grades, scores, and recommendations can tell us about any candidate. Please use the space on the back of this page to let us know something about you that we might not learn from the rest of your application."

"This is your opportunity to tell us about yourself. What would you most like the Admissions Committee to know about you in reading your application."

These questions boil down to "Tell us about yourself," a query you enjoyed answering when you had to devise a yearbook quotation. You weren't intimidated then—don't be now! The school just wants to know you better and see how you'll introduce yourself.

Advantages of This Question

1. It is direct. The college is asking you to add a clearer sense of you to your application. Remember, it's your best subject!

2. It is an open opportunity to speak for yourself, to plead your own case. If this is where you want to go to school, now is the time to put all you've got into letting them know that you're a "must admit" candidate. Your essay should reveal your personality, warmth, insight, and commitment.

Dangers of This Question

1. It is extremely open-ended. Remember that selection is the key. Find just one or two things that will reveal your best qualities. Focus is very important. (Use the essay process described in Chapter 5 to get a good focus.)
2. There is a temptation to default and tell everything, rather than focus on a single, illuminating point. Beware of the unedited autobiography.
3. Tone: You may feel self-conscious but you don't want to sound distant and academic. Some students use their stuffiest style and forget this is a personal essay. They think they ought to sound scholarly and write essays full of sentences like:

> Multitudinous homo sapiens in our contemporary culture are so engrossed in the trivia of material acquisition and success that they lose their intimate relationships with the essential elements of life—love, learning, and liberty. I myself am not one of those people.

Capitalize on the directness of this question and avoid the pitfalls. Look at yourself as a text, brainstorm and select an interpretation—one focus, one view of yourself—to send to the college. Then back it up with real and vivid events from your life that *prove* the interpretation you've chosen. Several strategies for doing this appear in Chapter 5.

Exploring the "Why Us?" Question

Some schools ask for an essay about your choice of school or career.

"How did you learn about NJIT and why are you applying for admission?" (New Jersey Institute of Technology)

"Why, in particular, do you wish to attend Bates?" (Bates College)

"What academic goals would you like to accomplish while at Clark?" (Clark University)

"How does the University of Chicago, as you know it now, satisfy your desire for a particular kind of learning, community, and future? Your response should address with some particularity your own wishes and how they relate to Chicago." (University of Chicago)

"Assess your reasons for wanting to attend college. How have your previous experiences influenced your current academic and/or career plans?"

Here, the college is looking for information about your educational direction and career goals. They also want to get an idea of how much you know about them, what research you've put into your choice process, and how serious your commitment is to this particular school.

Advantages of This Question

1. It is directly about you, an area in which you have great expertise.
2. You will not have difficulty finding something to write about. You have already been through the business of selecting schools and choosing X over Y; your reasons and choices are familiar and settled.
3. The focus is provided: why you chose the school. The proof is right in the catalog.
4. It is very important to understand where you're going and why. Bennington's study of successful students found that intelligence, emotional stability, and *a solid knowledge of Bennington and its philosophy* made their students succeed. Clearly, the information used in your answer is as important to you as it is to your application.

Dangers of This Question

1. You might not know your subject thoroughly enough. If you've chosen New York University because you want to be close to urban night life, this says something about your academic commitment. If you're going to Lewis & Clark to major in dance, the school can tell how carefully you've chosen (Lewis & Clark doesn't have a dance major).
2. Again, tone can be a problem. You want to be neither arrogant nor self-effacing. Rather than trying to flatter the reader, show a concrete knowledge of the school. Bernard Ravina, a successful applicant to Columbia, cautions, "Don't compliment the school outrageously … sniveling is not good for you and it is not good for the impression you are trying to create." Nancy Donehower says, "Too many kids give an ingratiating answer drawn from the catalog. It's insincere and it doesn't fool anybody."

Know the college and say, in a matter-of-fact way, why it is the one for you. This is your focus. Don't forget the proof, your specific and factual knowledge of the college's programs and special advantages. Name names, course offerings, professors, facilities. Make a clear and vivid connection between you and the school. Chapter 5 offers two strategies for dealing with this question.

Understanding the Creative Question

The last kind of question provides a more creative outlet for your response. Instead of trying to get a look at you through your choice of school, the colleges that use creative questions try to evaluate you through your choice of some tangential item: a national issue, a famous person, what you would put in a time capsule, a photograph.

"If you could travel through time and interview a prominent figure in the arts, politics, religion, or science, for example, whom would you choose and why?"

"Tell us about a teacher who has had a significant impact on your intellectual growth. How?"

"Of all the books you have read, which has made the deepest impression on you? Why?"

"Ask and answer the one important question that you wish we had asked."

"Please attach a photograph of something that has special meaning for you. Explain your choice."

"Explain why a particular day in the recent past continues to be important to you."

This, too, is an essay about you. The school is looking at your creativity and the breadth of your knowledge and education. They may find out if you read the papers, or just listen to five minutes of news when your favorite rock station takes a break. They may find out what you've read and how much you've thought about it. They may also find out if you can put yourself into an imaginary situation.

Advantages of This Question

1. A focus is provided. The range of your answer is somewhat limited by the question's designation of a hero, book, or national issue. You have something to react to.

2. The creative part of this question can help you with your proof, the evidence of the "you" that you're sending them. This is actually not such a hard question because the proof is easy to find once you've chosen your focus.

3. It can actually be fun! Your focus is you as an artist? Send a photo of your work or have lunch with Renoir. Your focus is the creative you? Send an X-ray of yourself or nominate Adam Sandler as Man of the Year.

Dangers of This Question

1. *The essay without substance.* Some seniors forget the importance of substantiation and write an uninformed essay. Don't write about lunch with a famous writer and get the titles of his or her novels wrong. Don't nominate Yoweri Museveni as Man of the Year if you haven't been following the politics of Africa. Research, as with the choice of school, can make a difference.

   In general, watch out for the national and international issues questions; it's very hard to be well informed. There's nothing wrong with an essay on South Africa or world hunger, if these are true concerns of yours. The rest of your application will support your choice. The problem is the insincere and therefore vague essay. Don't try to write "what they want to hear." Write about your real concerns; it's more revealing and a lot easier. A general and predictable piece of noble prose is a wasted effort if it lacks substance.

2. *The essay without sense.* Some seniors forget their purpose and write a crazy essay. Doubtless, truly creative essays can be very effective since popular topics are "safe" and therefore a little boring. Some admissions personnel, like Carol Lunkenheimer at Northwestern, say they would like to read "more quirky essays." Don Heider, at Albright College, thinks, "A risk is worth it for the 'reach' school."

Taking risks is a good idea but let common sense (and a few editors, readers, friends) be your guide. Admissions personnel may complain about too many "safe" essays, but risky essays can backfire. Vulgarity is never a good idea, and eccentricity can be dangerous. Some essays have stuck in readers' minds so tenaciously that they were unable to form a balanced judgment of the applicant's strengths. A fine applicant to an Ivy League school began his essay, "I am a racist, a sexist, and a bigot." It was hard to imagine why that essay was there; it was hard to forget. His high school record was memorable; his application was rejected.

The creative element is a problem for many students. They forget everything they know about writing and stray off the path by neglecting substance or sense.

We are not all creative souls. Few 17-year-olds can write like Toni Morrison or Dave Barry. Few adults can! The eccentric essay is a real challenge and a risk; don't rush to that option too quickly. It's a gamble that could pay off . . . or bankrupt you.

Counselors may steer you away from certain topics. But the colleges think otherwise: "In the past, candidates have used this space in a great variety of ways . . . There is no 'correct' way to respond to this essay request. . . ." No answer is wrong—but sloppy, general, insincere, or tasteless responses hurt. The travelog, the national or international issue, and autobiography may be too extensive and therefore too general. But some of the best essays, the memorable and unusual ones, are about very similar, *just more focused,* topics.

Essays about your family, football team, trip to France, parents' divorce, or twin can be effective as long as they're focused and specific: a single Christmas Eve church service, a meal of boiled tongue in Grenoble, dipping ice cream on a summer job. The best essay I ever read, whose author went to Yale, then to Oxford on a Rhodes scholarship, and then to a Wall Street brokerage house, was about the author's experience on the football team. Joyce Vining Morgan, at the Putney School in Vermont, counsels, "*Real* thinking is readable even if the topic is a common one."

The point is NO LEGITIMATE TOPIC IS WRONG! Use your head, be sincere, and treat anything you write about with specifics and focus. Chapter 5 suggests some different approaches for all of these questions.

Other Essay Problems

What if they give me only two inches in which to answer?

Some colleges—Kenyon, Barnard, Princeton, University of Pennsylvania, Lewis & Clark among many others—ask for only a paragraph's answer to one of these questions.

Others ask for an essay on one topic and designate other topics for paragraph answers. These questions are mini-essays and should be approached with the same care and attention you gave to the Big Essay. The colleges are asking you to do the same work as other schools only to condense it all into an inch or two instead of a page or a page and a half. Use the paragraph format discussed in Chapter 3. The process, however, is the same as that described in Chapter 5. Just reduce the introduction and conclusion to a sentence each. Try to make your topic vivid in a few lines—and never sacrifice specifics.

Here's a simple answer to a simple question. The application asked, "What has been your most important activity outside the classroom?" The applicant used 10 sentences to create a nuanced and effective picture of a part-time job. Surprisingly, often it is easier to write five pages on an Alice Munro story than five genuinely interesting sentences on that same subject. Don't overlook questions that ask for only a few sentences. Make the most of the *little* opportunities.

> The place I have learned the most from is the little pizza shop around the corner from my house where I have spent so much time working over the past two years. My most valuable lessons have come from dealing with difficult customers, working with fellow employees who are less than perfect but related to the boss, and scrubbing the grease off pans late at night when I have an English paper to

tackle, but am still 45 minutes from closing time. I have learned that being the outsider, whether in a family-run business or on a larger scale, is not fun, easy, or something that can be changed. I have learned that things often do not work out fairly. I have learned that often I will deserve without receiving and, as bad as that is, it is better than receiving without deserving. I have learned that an understanding smile is worth more than a large tip. Finally, I have learned that hard work isn't fun, but it's the only way to get what you need and feel good about it. Hard work isn't something to be admired; it is something that's expected. And its reward will come...eventually.

The principle is the same, regardless of the length of your answer. You may even want to write 500 words in response to these questions and then cut to the core, to the best 100 words, so only the most direct and clearest point is left.

What kind of writing sample should I send?

Some schools require or encourage submission of an academic essay or writing sample. There is no reason not to send a school essay. As you saw in Chapter 3, a lot of college writing is similar to what is done in high school. Choose a strong performance (a B + or better) and a paper on a not-too-esoteric topic. Do not send a 15-page term paper or a collation of library research. A short, illuminating essay on one poem, one lab experiment, one incident in history, is a good choice. Have a little consideration for your reader and send the original (if your handwriting is good), a typed copy (if it's not), or a high-quality photocopy. And try to send a paper with a fair number of teacher comments. These show how hard you've worked and how demanding your teachers have been. Poetry and creative writing are options also. But most high school seniors do not have enough writing experience to produce first-rate poetry and fiction. Unless you've won an award or received some other type of outside encouragement for your work, stick with a good expository essay of three to five pages.

Summary

There are many kinds of applications but essentially only three types of questions, all of which are meant to reveal how you choose. The key to success for all of them is to choose a clear *focus* and then *prove* your choice. If you can persuade your readers, you have won the day. Prove you're a creative person, prove you belong at the college to which you're applying, prove that the world needs a better mousetrap. The proof is the key.

Also, remember that although the essay should reveal information not found elsewhere in the application, it is part of a larger pattern emerging from your application. The essay about M. Lapardieu, who shaped your life and made French exciting, may not seem very original, but it will connect to straight A's in Advanced Placement French and a teacher recommendation from the head of the language department. Your choice of Case Western Reserve and your plans for a career in nursing will be corroborated by good grades in science and work at the local hospital. An essay on the space shuttle in an application with nothing else about astrophysics or the sciences may raise more questions than it answers. It is the proof that makes a choice valid, worthwhile, insightful. Only the essays with a clear focus and specific proof convey the best *you* to the admissions committee.

Quick Fixes for the First Paragraph

Start Strong

There are no wrong topics and no unredeemable beginnings. But here are some opening lines that make the business of writing a good application essay even harder than it has to be:

"I entered onto the scene of this terrestrial sphere on a vernal evening in 1985."

This is not a vocabulary test: try "I was born in April of 1985."

"I am my bedroom."

You are a lot more than some Gap clothes and a bunch of posters. Don't force yourself to be clever.

"The day my golden retriever died, my world changed. As Brandy's eyes closed…"

Even great writers—like Shakespeare, Frost, Allende—have struggled to say something meaningful and true about death. When you can write about anything, why choose the toughest topic in the world?

"My favorite book was *Wuthering Heights* by Jane Eyre."

Whoops … get your facts straight.

"In contemplating the invention that has had the greatest impact on human history, I would select the pet rock. Why you might ask would I select this seemingly mundane and trivial object …"

What seems original and funny to one person may seem predictable, studied, and boring to another. This idea might soar or it might crash. Get a second opinion from a disinterested adult before you submit an essay that you think is comical; even Letterman has a staff of writers.

Start Fast

Engage the reader with a quick start, rather than a slow stroll, into the topic; cutting or shrinking the first paragraph is almost always a strategy for improvement. Here is a ruthless revision of an introduction, meant to eliminate every unnecessary word and shift the burden of the discussion into the body of the essay. Of course, it's painful to delete even one of your own words, but self-editing is usually subtraction, not addition. By eliminating 123 words, the author loses a lot of "I" sentences and gains half a page for more specific incidents and reflections.

First draft

Three delicious meals a day, and a beautiful house to live in. It amazes me how much I take for granted. I never thought of how other people around the world were living, until I visited the home country of my parents, Bangladesh, in 1998 for the first time. To this day I can still remember how people were starving for food and freezing on the streets. The visit was an experience of a lifetime, and it changed my life forever. My visit to Bangladesh was intertwined with another first experience as well. I had never experienced a death in my family. My uncle, whom I was very close to, passed away that year, and he had asked to be buried back home. It was for this reason that my family had traveled to Bangladesh in the first place. I was hit with two emotional milestones at once: the death of my uncle and the experience of seeing a kind of life I had never witnessed before.

First revision

In 1998, for the first time, I visited the home country of my parents, Bangladesh, to attend the funeral of my uncle who had asked to be buried back home. I found there both a death and a life I had never witnessed before.

Chapter 5

Focusing on You

Contrasting Two Essays

Essay 1

Throughout my high school years, there have been many factors that have influenced my interests and personality. Being a
well-rounded student, I have had many experiences working
with people as well as with books. I have learned a great deal
through these experiences.

A major influence in my life has been my family. Their love
and encouragement have motivated me to expand in many
areas of interest.

Another factor that has influenced me is my involvement
in many activities outside of academics. Working with my
peers in musicals, tennis, dance class, volunteer work and
various committee and staff work, I have gained a sense
of achievement and accomplishment. I have learned to work
better with people, learning the value of team effort.
I have gained an appreciation for the talent and hard
work contributed by each and every person concerned
with the project.

Working in Maine during the past few summers, I have learned much about dealing with people in a great variety of situations. My co-employees, being older than I am, also helped me to mature and accept things as they are. Furthermore, I now know more about the economic aspect of life, both business and personal.

In college, I plan to continue to live a well-rounded life, meeting and working with people from a variety of backgrounds. I expect to prepare for a profession that permits me to be closely related to children as well as adults. I want to help people. I have gotten so much out of life through the love and guidance of my family, I feel that many individuals have not been as fortunate; therefore, I would like to expand the lives of others.

I am excited about the possibility of attending [College X]. I feel that I am ready for college. I am ready to accept the challenge of the academics. I plan to give my best to [College X], knowing that [College X] will do the same for me.

This is the kind of essay admissions personnel read all day long. It is not, however, the kind of essay they remember, nor the kind that sends a "gray zone" application to the committee for reconsideration. At a highly competitive school, it's the kind of essay that might be classified D.O.A. (dead on arrival). Most important of all, this is not the kind of essay you want to write.

William Hiss, at Bates, calls these "Boy Scout" essays. They describe an ideal student—eager, involved, loyal, thrifty, reverent—but it's a general picture, not a real person. The college can't make use of this kind of picture. (In fact, many colleges rethink and revise their questions every year, hoping to broaden the range of responses and reduce the number of predictable or "safe" essays they receive. The University of Chicago's questions have excited and challenged applicants in different ways every year since 1983.)

This essay does not add to the application because it is unfocused and too general; it could apply to any high school senior. Okay, you didn't summer in Maine. Make that California or any place in between.

And you were more interested in lacrosse and the yearbook than tennis, dance, and the school musicals. Change the college's name to the school of your choice and you're all set. Three changes. Whatever else this essay has going for it, it can't do much for the author if three changes could make it yours. It wastes the opportunity to convey to the admissions committee a fresh and vital sense of the writer.

Essay 2

Someday, I hope to have a career in the biological sciences. I've always enjoyed the study of science, with its plausible explanations for the 'hows' and 'whys' of our lives. My serious interest in the area of the sciences developed in my sophomore year, during which I took Advanced Placement biology. One aspect of that course I particularly enjoyed was the final project of designing, conducting, and writing up my own experiment.

Although the work involved was time-consuming, doing the experiment allowed me to see how real scientists test hypotheses. My laboratory dealt with the effects of photoperiod and temperature on the growth of zea mays seedlings. Not only did I have to care for and daily alter the photoperiods of the plants, I also had to measure, every other day, the heights of 76 corn seedlings. As the labs were to be researched and prepared on a college level, I spent several hours in the library at Washington University and Meramec College, using the Biological Abstracts to find information on experiments similar to my own which had been written up in scientific journals. The effort required by the lab really made me appreciate the scientists who spend their lives proving or disproving theories by experimentation and research.

Ironically, the experiment was personally rewarding because my original theory was actually disproved. I hypothesized that the plants with the longest photoperiod would grow the fastest. After I concluded the lab and began analyzing the data, however, I found that the plants with a median photoperiod grew faster. I thought that this was very exciting; potentially routine results were given a twist.

I consider my biology experiment to be a valuable scientific experience; I was exposed to the methods and materials of bona fide scientists, and, in a small way, felt the excitement of discovery. That laboratory intensified my interest in science. Last year, in chemistry, I conducted more self-designed experiments, including one to test the amount of copper in copper chloride, and another to determine the amount of oxygen required for survival by a fish, a mussel, and a clam. These experiments were also worthwhile, but I still consider the *zea mays* experiment to be the most exciting lab I've ever done.

A sense of this girl—her way of looking at the world, her involvement and enthusiasm—comes across. Unless you took Advanced Placement biology, did a corn experiment, read *Biological Abstracts*, learned about scientific research, and made connections between your work in that class, other classes, and your career plans, you couldn't write this particular essay. Its strengths are its clear focus (the Advanced Placement experiment) and its specifics (the class, the 76 seedlings, *Biological Abstracts*, Meramec, copper chloride, the clam). These make it memorable and unique. According to Margit Dahl, director of admissions at Yale, "We want a strong and well-developed personal point of view, not an institutional response." The *focus* and *proof* are what distinguish this essay. In Essay 1, the writer assures us that her family is supportive, that she learned a lot in Maine, and that she wants to help people. But there's no evidence of any of that. In Essay 2, the writer *shows* her points. She says she enjoyed the study of science, and the 76 seedlings prove it.

Most college essays fail on one of these counts: They're either too comprehensive (no focus) or too general (no proof). Those with no focus are the autobiographies and the travelogs; those with no proof are the "Boy Scout" essays. Regardless of which essays you have to write, you want them to be personal, to be distinctively yours; to accomplish this, you must write focused and specific responses.

Prewriting: Creating a Self-Outline

Step 1: Brainstorm and Ask Questions

Begin with YOU. As explained in Chapter 4, the questions are all attempts to learn about you. Follow the basic writing process reviewed in Chapter 3: prewrite, draft, edit. These steps are as useful for a college application essay as they are for an English paper on *Hamlet*. The text just happens to be you. So begin with you.

Start by brainstorming. Sit down with paper and pencil and fill a page with statements about yourself. List things you've done, places you've been, accomplishments you're proud of. Set a timer or a time limit and write until the page is full. Write down everything you can think of about yourself: the good, the bad, the special, the obvious, the habitual, the extraordinary. Don't consider your audience at this point. This performance is just for you.

If you have followed the plan in Chapter 2, you have plenty of time. Keep a journal for a few weeks if your brainstorming is going nowhere. Record not what you do each day but your responses and thoughts about each day's experiences. This can be a valuable source of insights and ideas about yourself. Or collect "important moment" articles and interviews from magazines and newspapers. Sports figures and celebrities often recount small but enlightening incidents in their lives in response to interviewers' questions. Or use the résumé you created for your guidance counselor and recommending teachers. You can make an activities list or résumé now if you haven't done so already. Add it all to your brainstorm sheet.

Ask yourself questions: "What are my strengths? My weaknesses?" Do a little soul-searching and be as complete as possible. Add evaluative statements like "I am a stubborn person" or "I like a challenge." Be totally honest.

Now research your topic a little. There aren't any Cliffs Notes and there's nothing in the public library. But you can look over your journal or an old scrapbook or photo album, and talk to your parents, friends, and employer. Gather ideas about yourself wherever you can. Ask yourself why you do the things you do. What drives you out the front door at 6 a.m. to run five miles? What keeps you up past midnight trying to build a computer program? Ask yourself: What is special about me? What kind of person am I? Under what circumstances do I learn? What interests me? What do I care about? Why is swimming, to me, more a religion than a sport? What is it like growing up in Jerome, Idaho . . . or Needham, Massachusetts . . . or Glendale, Missouri?

Do not do this in 15 minutes one Sunday afternoon. Begin well in advance of the drafting stage and really percolate your topic. A special fringe benefit of taking the college essay seriously is that it can be a learning experience, not just for the college, but for you, too.

Step 2: Focus

Making connections is the next step. You need to analyze your topic and divide it into some manageable pieces. As you saw in the *Simpsons* sample in Chapter 3, grouping similar ideas and events together highlights patterns in a miscellaneous collection of information. For example, is there a series of volunteer projects? Does your love of math show up in your performance in the state math competition and in your summer job at the computer store? Ask yourself more questions to establish connections, clusters, and groups.

Now focus on three or four important strengths. Keep the unusual, the individual, the vivid. Be positive ("stubborn" isn't a great quality, but "committed" is), and don't be afraid of the truth; being honest is the only way to get a fresh and sincere result.

Step 3: Prove

Remember, this is an essay. Your purpose is to persuade the readers of a particular view or interpretation of your subject. That applies as much to a paper on *The House on Mango Street* as to a paper on you. The first requires specific evidence from the novel. The college essay requires evidence from your life.

Organize your information into a self-outline. List personality characteristics, and under each list five or six pieces of evidence from your life, things you've been or done, that validate your point. Each characteristic is a potential focus for your essay, and you need to see which ones are important, which ones you can say something about.

The evidence is crucial. If you've said you're concerned with the welfare of others but can't think of more than one proof, omit it. You're not really motivated by concern for others. You thought you *ought* to be, you thought the college would like to hear that you are. But this is an example of the "institutional response." Forget it!

Look for a potentially interesting and rich focus. As you might toy with opinions about a novel's characters, setting, or foreshadowing techniques, experiment with ideas about your own goals, interests, or style. Then see what things have happened to you and what things you have done that support or illuminate these preliminary thesis statements.

Your self-outline might include items like:

1. I like to work with kids
   a. Community House
   b. my little brother
   c. babysitter and mother's helper
   d. Christmas pageant for the church
   e. career interest in child psychology

2. I like classes with student participation
   a. Mr. Stivers' class
   b. drama workshop
   c. Ms. Selman's class

3. I hate sports
   a. gym is dumb
   b. in fourth grade I never got picked for a team
   c. the field hockey jocks are weird (stupid head-bands, weird socks)
   d. I've got enough competition in my life already
   e. I'm uncoordinated (falling off the parallel bars in seventh grade in front of Andrea Kaufman)

4. I always put things off until right before the deadline
   a. this essay
   b. my tenth-grade research paper
   c. getting my yearbook quote done
   d. prom table

Time for more questions. About what have you written the most? What looks interesting, different (but not unflattering)? Are there any career goals here? Motivations for college? Special personal characteristics or experiences? Working with kids might be interesting if your career and college choice are related. The preference for classes with student participation might make a good essay in applying to a college with seminar classes. Certainly a loathing for sports is an interesting point. But where can you go with it? Can you use it to show something positive about yourself (maybe your individuality?), something other than just eccentricity or negativity? The procrastination habit is probably not something you want to share with the college; it should be overcome, not glorified.

Again, remember there are no right answers for these questions any more than for any other essay. Admissions committees are diverse groups of individuals; there isn't one particular thing they want to hear. After reading 20 to 50 essays a day about the charms of University X, the evils of terrorism, and the personal commitment involved in being a doctor, most admissions staffers don't want more essays on "safe" topics. How things are in Paramus, New Jersey, or New Hope, Alabama, might be more engaging. "Schools would rather have a sense of the student's place in the world, a sense of his or her relationship—context—as a person," says Chicago-based educational consultant Betsy DeLaHunt.

Looking for the "right" answers is therefore pointless. And it is also counterproductive. The college essay is not an assignment to create a self. "We don't want the back lot at MGM, a created scene over a barren field. We want to see the real landscape," says Bates's Bill Hiss.

When the time comes to write, don't try to find the "right answers." And don't stare at the blank paper and despair. Stare at your self-outline. This prewriting is a good launching pad. By writing about yourself in this format, you will have a beginning, and "begun is half done." Don't cheat on this step. Give it plenty of time and attention. Write to write. It will pay off when the drafting begins.

Drafting: Converting the Self-Outline into an Essay

Now consider your questions. With a self-outline, you can plan and create any of the three types of essays required. Several strategies are given for each question. Take your choice. There is no one right answer, no one right essay. Just remember: FOCUS AND PROVE!

Question 1: "Tell Us About Yourself"

Strategy 1: A Standard Essay with Several Well-Proven Points

The most conservative essay about yourself would be based on two or three of the points from your self-outline and would follow a standard introduction/body/conclusion plan. Look back at this chapter's sample Essay 1. The writer attempted one paragraph on family, one on activities, and one on jobs. It is, in fact, a well-organized essay. There is an introduction that identifies the points to be discussed, one point for each body paragraph, and a conclusion that relates the writer to the college. But although the essay's organization is very good, its weakness is a lack of specifics.

If you choose to write this type of essay, select two or three points from your self-outline, give a paragraph to each, and be sure you give plenty of evidence. Don't try to do too much: two or at most three points should do it. Either choose things not apparent from the rest of your application or "light up" some of the activities and experiences listed there. Make it vivid. The difference between general (and forgettable) and specific (and interesting) can be seen in the following first and final drafts of one paragraph from a student's essay.

Example 1

The job I had this past summer expanded my level of maturity and provided me with exposure to a world that I had not previously experienced. It involved a combination of a job as doorman and a custodial worker in a New York apartment building. This job allowed me to break out of my shell and see the spectrum of the world as a whole. I have learned balance and adaptability. And I can empathize with the hard-working people of the so-called lower class for many of them are now my friends.

Example 2

The job I had this past summer introduced me to physical labor and some new attitudes. I worked a forty-hour week as a doorman and custodian at the Renoir, an apartment building with 120 units on East 78th Street in Manhattan. I had a black tuxedo with a striped vest for half my day and, for the rest of the day, a paint-spattered blue and white jumpsuit that said 'Howie' on the pocket. In either outfit, I often found I was ignored by the people I helped. I got a little more acknowledgment in the tuxedo. I never got a 'Hello' but I did get a few 'Thank you's' from the people I held the door for. As the custodian, I was invisible. I could go four or five hours without hearing a single word directly addressed to me. From this job, I think I learned something about New York, about furnaces, and about the human temperament when deprived of air conditioning. But I also learned something about how our society treats people who do manual labor.

There's nothing wrong with a standard essay about yourself; just give plenty of time to building up and making specific the paragraph development that proves each of your points. Do not substitute a list of activities for support. Make a point about yourself in each paragraph and then present evidence to illuminate it, to back it up.

Strategy 2: Less Is More

For many years, Yale suggested applicants write an essay about interests, activities, background, or aspirations; they got a lot of four-paragraph essays, with one paragraph for interests, one for activities, one for background, and one for aspirations. They changed their question to avoid this "laundry list" kind of response.

You might want to draft a standard essay (Strategy 1) and then mine it for the most interesting and important point about yourself. This is especially useful if your essay is supposed to be one paragraph or half a page. Essay 1, at the beginning of this chapter, distilled to its best and most vivid paragraph, could be very effective. The writer wanted to explain the importance of her family, but she tried to do it in only two sentences! She might have done better with an essay on just that one idea—her family's support. She could have used her page to *show* the half inch of rain that fell on her first varsity field hockey game (and on her mother and father). To this picture of soggy family devotion she might have tied her extracurricular involvement and the source of her own commitment to help others. There's a lot to be said for taking a small focus and really *showing* it to the reader.

The student who wrote about his summer job also ended up using a "less is more" strategy. He had originally begun with an essay of several paragraphs—one for clubs, one for sports, one for jobs (Example 1), and one for career plans. The final essay focused only on the summer job and tied it to several other revealing points. Drafting helped him identify the best point; other ideas were subordinated to it. He ended up with two strong paragraphs (one given in Example 2) instead of four flabby ones. (See Sample 6 in Chapter 7 for a personal essay that focuses on five minutes of summer work.)

Cleopatra had herself delivered to Julius Caesar rolled up in an Oriental carpet. I imagine it was a rather memorable delivery. The "less is more" essay makes a vivid self-presentation from within a simple (even ordinary) framework.

Strategy 3: The Narrative Essay

The most focused and narrow approach to the "Tell us about yourself" question is a short and vivid story. Omit the introduction, write one or two narrative paragraphs that grab and engage the reader's attention, then show how this little tale reveals you. Sample 3 in Chapter 7 uses something like this strategy. The writer begins with an introduction, then tells the story of a conversation from which he draws a picture of himself, his background, his insights. This type of essay puts the proof first and the focus last. See Sample 7 in Chapter 6. It's a little more risky but it can be very interesting. If you're a good writer, give it a try; if not, rely on a more conservative strategy.

Your procedure for the "You" question is:

1. Ask questions to create a self-outline.
2. Focus on several of your distinctive qualities.
3. Prove what you say with extensive and vivid evidence.
4. Use several proofs or a fully described incident for each body paragraph; do not write a list of activities, a travelog, or an autobiography. Avoid pure chronology.
5. Choose one of the following:
   - a standard essay with several equal focus points in several well-developed body paragraphs
   - a "less-is-more" essay that uses one experience to make several points
   - a short narrative that leads to your focus

6. BE SPECIFIC! None of these styles of a "tell-us-about-yourself" essay will hurt you as long as you remember to make it concrete, detailed, vivid.

Question 2: "Why Did You Select College X?"

The focus and the proof for "Why Us?" questions are provided: The focus is the connection between you and the school, and the proof is on the campus and in the catalog. Review the pluses of the school and how you came to choose it. Find connections between the college and the points on your self-outline. Then decide what percentage of the essay ought to treat the school and what percentage ought to treat you.

Strategy 1: A Standard Essay on the School's Pluses

Using the standard introduction/body/conclusion format, you can write an essay whose body paragraphs are the points about the school that are attractive to you as a prospective first-year. Do some research. Read the course catalog and viewbook carefully, surf the Web site, and

see what is offered that appeals to you. From this you can focus on the main connection between you and the school. Your body might begin with one paragraph on small points—location, climate, size, the composition of the student body—and build to one or two paragraphs on the more significant factors—curriculum offerings, class settings (tutorials, conferences, mass lectures), majors, special programs.

If you're sure of your career goal, make this your thesis; then show what the school has to offer in your particular area of concentration. Be sure they do have what you need and want. This is as important for you as it is for them. Is the faculty first rate? (Ask friends or teachers about the faculty roster.) Are there some well-known people in your field teaching there? Does the library have a unique section devoted to American political science, Judaica, the letters of W.E.B. DuBois? Do some research and mention specific factors that tie in with your primary interest. For example, if you plan to concentrate in international relations, you might mention the college's Chinese language and literature program, its Junior Year Abroad option, or the short-term work-study program at the United Nations.

Avoid an ingratiating tone. Instead, prove whatever you say. Point out the real advantages of a particular school or program.

> I've always wanted to work in the health care field. But how I want to do this is still not clear to me. That's why Georgetown's nursing and health studies school appeals to me. I want at least a B.S.N., rather than just an R.N. I don't want to feel "different" from the rest of the under-graduate body, and I like the idea of mixed undergraduate housing. And the nursing/pre-medical option also seems right for me since I am still considering medical school.

It's to your advantage as a potential freshman to scrutinize the place where you will live for four years, become an adult, and spend in excess of $100,000. Your answer, paragraph or essay, should show your interest and prove the school's distinctiveness in that area. It will become apparent if a school was chosen whimsically or because your boyfriend is a junior there. Dig in, find out, and then use your knowledge.

Strategy 2: The School and You

Some colleges ask for an essay that connects you to them:

"Assess your reasons for wanting to attend college. How have your previous experiences influenced your current academic and/or career plans?"

This is an essay primarily about you. It asks only secondarily about your choice of college. Write a personal essay as suggested in Strategy 1 or 2 of the "Tell Us About Yourself" question. Then use the conclusion to make a connection to the college. The second type of conclusion discussed in Chapter 3, one that serves as a springboard for further ideas, may be helpful here.

In sample Essay 1 on page 87 the writer set out to show the importance of her college choice in her conclusion, but there was no substance to her paragraph. Had she mentioned the college's preprofessional studies in law or its special 3–2 program in nursing she would have created a real connection between her plans to help others and her choice of college. Wherever you show why College X is for you, be specific and well informed.

Your procedure for the "Why Us" question is:
1. Ask questions to create a self-outline.
2. Research the college for the qualities that make it special to you. Know the facts.
3. Connect yourself to the college. Select one of the following:
   - Make several body paragraphs from these connections, building toward the most important ones.
   - Write an essay about yourself that comes to the *conclusion* that X is the college for you.
4. Research is the key to good proof; highlight *real* connections between you and the college.
5. Avoid an ingratiating tone. BE SPECIFIC.

Question 3: Be Creative

Strategy 1: Begin with You

If you have a creative question, there is again some built-in help. If you've been directed to write about a roommate, book, or photo, consult your self-outline and with a suitable focus select the topic that corresponds to a particular quality of yours.

If you're artistic, have lunch with Georgia O'Keeffe and make your conversation with her reveal your interests in art. If you're a violin virtuoso, nominate Anne-Sophie Mutter for person of the year and *show* that you know why she deserves it. You're a creative soul? Send Vassar a photo of your SpongeBob SquarePants Halloween costume. In an essay about the creation of the outfit and other similar activities, *show* them you have the imagination and skills to conceive and execute other original ideas. Harvard liked an application essay about chocolate; the writer used her job in a candy store to show her insight, judgment, and creativity.

You can use a standard essay form here. The focus is your choice. Your body paragraphs should describe the pleasures of that book, the imagined invention, or the three major changes you would enact at your high school. Again, remember that it is the specifics that will make or break this essay. Sample 2 in Chapter 7 fails not because of the author's topics, but because he offered little concrete knowledge of them. Read up a little on your dinner guest, review that novel you've chosen, talk to your high school principal. Your initiative and sincerity will show in the specificity of your end result.

Strategy 2: A Production Piece

Shakespeare said, "the poet's pen / Turns [things unknown] to shapes, and gives to airy nothing / A local habitation and a name." An essay may, likewise, in a variety of ways, give a "local habitation and a name" to you. A purely creative essay can reveal your imagination, willingness to take a risk, creativity, and insight. If the question is totally without limits, an imaginative piece may demonstrate the most about you.

Audrey Smith, at Smith College, says, "We hope to get a sense of the person, the individual. The vehicle can be almost anything." Thus, it is almost impossible to give advice here. It is helpful only to say that some students have found that a sense of themselves as individuals was most evident in an original piece—a meditation on their nickname, a speculation about elm trees, a hypothesis about socks (see Sample 5 in Chapter 7). It's risky, but for some students, it is the right risk and very effective. You're on your own with this one; good luck!

The procedure for the creative question is:

1. Ask questions to create a self-outline.
2. Choose a representative quality from the self-outline.
3. Connect this quality to a choice that will illuminate it: an artist if painting is important to you, the charms of J. M. Coetzee if you're a budding writer, and so on. Be sincere and do not try to choose "what you think they want."
4. Research your choice.
5. Write a SPECIFIC and vivid defense of your subject.
6. Get a second opinion.

Summary

A standard essay, well-organized and specific in its focus and proof, is a reasonable answer for any question. Neither predictable answers nor innovative choices make memorable essays unless you SHOW the rightness of the choice. Tiger Woods is a better choice than George W. Bush for man of the year only if you argue it persuasively. A very good case could be made for Bush, too, but only if you've got four great reasons and lots of evidence from specific events to back it up. FOCUS AND PROVE, no matter what!

The dangers are not in the topics themselves. When admissions people complain about travelogs and autobiographies, it is the lack of focus, the broad angle that is the downfall of these essays. When counselors advise students against responses about trips, sports, twins, divorces, it's because lack of proof, the generality of these essays, can be a problem. Memorable essays on any of these topics exist, by writers who took a narrow focus and backed it up with plenty of vivid specifics. Choose a strategy that feels comfortable and be specific.

The High-Risk Essay

Does the following dilemma sound familiar to you? "I'm about to apply to a school with 13,000 applicants and 1,300 places. Is it wise to aim for a big impact? I need a high-powered performance that's going to get me in!"

Keep in mind that, although the essay is important, no single aspect of the application can get you into a college. The essay can make a difference, but it is not sensible to believe that a knockout essay will get you into a school you're not generally qualified to attend. Don't try to do something that will "make up for all the rest" of your application—it will only lead to embarrassment and disappointment.

Okay, you are a qualified applicant for this school, but you need to stand out. You've decided you want to be different. You've had it with "safe" and decided you want to write an essay that is a "powerful tipper" for your case. Can it be done? Maybe.

Think of the Academy Awards. Well over a hundred people make similar acceptance speeches that night. What makes any of them stand out in our memories?

1. *Surprise* does. Some acceptance speeches say things we aren't expecting to hear. You could write about a point from your self-outline that few other writers would choose. For example, instead of writing about your concern for children, you could write about why you hate sports.

2. *Form* can do it. Some speakers surprise us not with what they say but with how they say it. A narrative essay may have enough suspense (if it isn't too long) to give this added element. The essay on a job in a candy store included a chocolate *Veritas* (Harvard's motto). It won't get an applicant accepted, but it is memorable.

3. The *unusual* can grab lagging attention. Special circumstances—and I mean really special—can make a distinctive essay. "When I first realized that my mother was deaf, it did not affect me much at all; my transactions between the deaf world and the hearing world had become a matter of course...."

    Supplementary materials may help here, too. The student who described a 250-toothpick bridge that supported 286 pounds and won him a physics competition made it real by sending the bridge along. But think a long time about sending support material. Send only something individual, of very high quality, and related to the total impact of your application. The toothpick bridge would not have enhanced the application if seven others were sent, if it had supported only eight pounds, or if the applicant wanted to become a music major. Research the admissions committee a little before you send anything. If faculty are involved, tapes, artwork, and projects may get more attention. But remember the volume of applications that have to be reviewed and don't expect more than your share of attention.

4. *Humor* usually works—*real* humor. A lot of high school humor is goofy, embarrassing, or in poor taste. Just remember Noel Coward's advice: "Wit ought to be a glorious treat, like caviar. Never spread it about like marmalade." Get a second (and a third) opinion.

5. And, of course, *shock* can do the job . . . either for or against you. You want to be clever not silly, a risk taker, not a fool. John Bunnell, associate dean and director of admission emeritus at Stanford, cautions that, "The problem is there's a thin line between being humorous and being flip, between being creative and being eccentric. Taking risks is not a negative quality, but there ought to be some common sense involved." Applicants who, given one day in time to spend with anyone in history, choose Britney Spears haven't thought much about their options. And please don't write about your first sexual experience.

You have to weigh the risk. Of course, there is often a high reward where there is a high risk. It takes something special to get a reader to say, "Hey, Alice, listen to this one!" And I am sure in the final hours of committee meetings on "gray zone" applications, no one has ever said, "Hey, wait a minute, what about that kid who wrote the essay about a *community service* project?"

But the predictable essay doesn't damn its author as much as a tasteless and vulgar attempt to astonish and surprise. Write about whatever makes you comfortable. Take a chance if that's your nature. You may find a like-minded individual on the committee who champions your application because of your essay. Whatever you write should be specific. And do get a couple of opinions on it; long hours at a desk can blur your sense of right versus ridiculous.

Editing

A Word About Computers

General Web sites like www.collegeboard.com, financial aid sites like www.fafsa.ed.gov, or the site for downloading the Common Application (www.commonapp.org) are wonderful resources. The sites of the colleges themselves provide names and numbers, deadlines, tour information, maps, downloadable forms, and extensive program information. You can e-mail questions from the "Contact Us" page on many of these sites or find the right coach or faculty member to query.

Word-processing skills should ease the business of writing your applications, and completing one version of the Common Application prepares you to file online to a multitude of colleges.

If you have followed the timeline suggested in Chapter 2 and are not working against an immediate deadline, begin an idea bank on a computer. Brainstorming may be a lot easier with a keyboard and screen than with pencil and paper, and any assignment benefits from the revision and editing capabilities of a computer.

You will draft, redraft, and edit the college essay many times, and you may want to recycle and revise it into several versions for different colleges. The computer allows you to make modifications quickly and painlessly and then, while saving the original version of your paper, to print a neat copy of the latest version without adding any new errors. You are more likely to write eight different essays truly tailored to each school if it's almost as easy to do as making eight copies of one essay. (And it's nice to have a built-in spell-checker to hunt down and identify your errors.)

If you don't own your own computer, investigate some of the following options after school:

- The high school writing center, library, or computer classroom
- A relative's office
- The local college library
- A computer center that charges by the hour for use of their equipment

A few words of caution. Proofread carefully. Neatly typed pages tend to look perfect when they often are not. Read drafts several times. Sometimes the thorny problem areas signaled in handwritten drafts by multiple cross-outs and arrows fail to stand out on typed pages. Read the copy on the screen and then in a final hard copy draft before the last printout. The typographical errors of a computer often are different from the traditional errors of a typewriter; reformatting problems, incomplete deletions, and misplaced insertions are the new kinds of errors to look for.

Don't procrastinate and believe the speed of the printer can buy time. Revising your Bryn Mawr essay for Dartmouth is a poor idea if you forget to delete references to the advantages of living in the Philadelphia area. No matter how you produce your essay, proofread it carefully several times.

Handwritten essays are harder to read, so do type if possible. If the application specifically asks, as some do, for your own handwriting, make sure it's legible and not crammed onto the page. I once had a student who had "dumb" handwriting. Lisa was very bright, but she had

big, loopy handwriting and she dotted her "i's" with cute little circles. I tried to explain to her that most people would pick up a paper like hers with a preconception that it was going to be a "C" performance at best. We finally agreed that typing her papers would free her from this subtle liability. Keep this in mind if you decide that typing takes too much time. You can always print out your essays and attach them to the application.

Editing Tips

No matter how you draft and write your essay, you will want to edit it. Remember your goal: to introduce yourself to the admissions committee. And remember your strategy: focus and prove. Reread your essay once to be sure you have zeroed in on one or two illuminating ideas about yourself and have shown them to your reader with plenty of specifics.

Then read the essay a second time. Look for spelling errors, sentence fragments, and confused expressions. Rewrite and revise. Some sentences cannot be improved and must be cut. When in doubt, strike it out.

Read the essay again for style.

1. Remember that good writing has a natural, easy-to-read quality. Keep the language and structure simple, direct, and clear. Don't try to hide shoddy thinking behind elaborate language. Use the fewest and simplest words possible.
2. Strike a balance between a personal and a formal tone. In a choice between a long, fancy word and a short, simple one, choose the simple word:
   a. The reason for this predicament is that the local hardware store does not have the extensive financial resources needed in order to be able to stock every size of every hardware item.
   b. Revised: Hardware stores can't afford much variety.

a. Having been involved in theater arts activities for many years, on a wide variety of levels ranging from high school to independent repertory theater, I have naturally gained a fairly comprehensive acting experience.

b. Revised: My knowledge of acting comes from high school productions and independent repertory theater work.

a. I have an intense affinity for learning in a liberal arts environment that has extensive course offerings from which to choose.

b. Revised: I want the choices that a liberal arts education offers.

The language used in the "a" samples distances the reader, something you do not want to do in your college essay. Avoid the thesaurus, be yourself, and don't substitute a stuffy style for substance.

3. Remember that your audience is the admission committee, not the English faculty's poet-in-residence or the chairman of the chemistry department. They are reading hundreds of applications. They are a group of individuals with individual ideas of what the college needs and wants. They are not scholars, and they are pressed for time. Be intelligent and knowledgeable, but above all, be yourself.

4. Avoid clichés and sentences that sound good but don't mean anything. For example, don't end with a line like, "I'll bring as much to College X as X will give to me." "To learn, to love, to live" sounds great—alliteration always sounds great—but it doesn't say much. Make every sentence count.

5. Avoid worn-out literary sources. Forget "to thine own self be true." Over-used quotations, old saws, and familiar maxims will sap the freshness out of your performance.

6. Don't inflate your credentials. Posting car wash signs does not qualify as "marketing director" for your church youth group. Using words carelessly or inaccurately will only hurt your chances.

7. Use active verbs and vigorous expression. Instead of "Due to my parents' coaxing, I decided to try once more" say "My parents coaxed me to try again." Instead of "My interest in sports was encouraged by my father" say "My father encouraged my football career."

8. Avoid empty words and phrases like "really," "special," "unique," "interesting," "each and every," and "meaningful."

9. Avoid vague and predictable conclusions: "I learned a lot," "I interacted with others different from myself," "I benefited from the love and support of my family," "I learned to work with others."

10. Proofread, proofread, proofread. The essay that began, "If there is one word that can describe me, that word is 'profectionist,'" did not make a favorable impression on the admissions committee at Bates. An admission staffer who graduated the previous June or a senior student intern may not disqualify you for grammatical errors, but why take the chance? Essays are read as an indication of writing skill. You might get the chairman of the English department as your reader!

Now put it all away for a week. Then reread it two more times for errors. Your essay doesn't have to win a Pulitzer Prize, but it should show both effort and commitment in its clarity, specificity, and correctness.

Making the Essay Yours

Colleges expect you to get some help with your essay. Your counselor might talk to you about choosing a subject, and your parents or a teacher might help proofread a final draft. These are legitimate steps of the drafting and editing processes, and all writers get some of this kind of help.

Ultimately, the application essay should be written under roughly the same circumstances that you will find in college. This doesn't include a full-time live-in editor/dad/counselor or a resident English teacher with a red pen. But it certainly can include friends to talk to, wise advisers to kick ideas around with, and a little friendly hands-off guidance from a teacher or mentor. Colleges provide writing centers, peer tutors, office hours, and advisers for just this purpose. Using similar resources for this important high school assignment is appropriate. While you're sitting on the eggs, waiting for your "idea" to hatch, parents, counselors, friends, and teachers can help you with the discourse of thinking. Choose someone who knows you and who can be honest with you. Friends qualify on the first count but aren't always objective or experienced enough to be helpful. And remember, in the end, only you can *write* your essay. Since the essay should introduce you to the college, no one else should speak for you but yourself.

Of course, there are sites from which to purchase or paste essays. And you may wonder, "If ordering pizza is an alternative to making dinner, then why can't I just download one of these essays?"

And of course, the answer is, "Because that's stealing."

"What if I make a bunch of changes—you know, *my* hometown in sentence two, *my* activities, *my* sport?"

Sorry. Just as you would not use someone else's SAT scores or falsify your grades, you must not include any part of a published work or another student's writing in your college essay. This is plagiarism and, if it is discovered, your application will be denied. Your high school will be informed, and all of your applications may be affected. Even if you're not caught, you have misrepresented yourself to the school. You don't want to end up at a college knowing that you got in on false pretenses.

Don't let someone else write your essay for you either. Do not use a service that offers to help you with your essay "line by line, if needed," for a fee. Colleges are not the enemy anxious to find a reason to deny you admission. As a general rule, the right credentials for the right school will not be ignored. The majority of schools in this country accept 50 percent or more of their applicants. You and the school are in a cooperative process of "mating." Misrepresenting yourself cannot help; it's neither satisfying nor mature. If you are ready to go to college, then you are ready to accept your successes and failures as your own. Believe in yourself and tell your own story.

Summary

No matter what questions you have to answer, begin with yourself. Brainstorm and focus on one or two points that will introduce and illuminate you to the admissions committee.

Then select your strategy. Write a short, legible, and correct essay, standard or varietal, that *shows* the qualities about you that you have chosen to illuminate with vivid specifics, not generalities.

Revise, proofread, and type it up. Photocopy your various application packets and mail off the originals. Check with your recommending teachers and with the guidance office to be sure they've contributed their share. Then relax. If you've followed the timeline and the steps outlined in this book, once the colleges to which you've applied have made their decisions, you will probably have the luxury of yet another opportunity to choose.

Quick Fixes for Procrastinators

Okay, asking questions and brainstorming and finding the inner "you" sounds good but it's Thanksgiving weekend, and you are locked in your room with no clue about a topic. Emergency!

All the strategies described above haven't made it easy, and now your primary inspiration is the deadline. Here are some last-minute strategies:

1. Look around your room. Pick three things you plan to take to college with you (or wish you could). Write three sentences that explain why that poster, that chunk of rock, that photograph matter to you. Then see if one of these things might be the beginning of an essay about an event or a person that has had significance in your life.

2. Find a family picture album. Spend an hour looking through it. What images stand out in your mind? What events were depicted? Wait...don't write about learning to ride a bike or graduating from kindergarten. Try to find a thread of interest—a renewed friendship, a magic place, a person who keeps showing up at the important moments. Then see what you have to say about the influence of that person or place.

3. Go find a parent. Ask them what they think are your strengths and talents. Ask what "kind" of person they think you are. What characteristics and talents do they think you should mention? (If you want to be really mean, ask *them* to write an essay about *you*.) Don't fail to exploit the knowledge of a person who's spent 17 years with you (and who really likes you).

4. Go find your favorite teacher or coach. Ask them where they think you should go to college and then why they chose that place. Ask them to help you remember exactly what it is you contribute to a group; then think about a specific time when that was evident in their class or on their team.

5. Go back to any journal or portfolio assignment you've done for school. How have you changed since you did this work? Does it still interest you? If yes, consider talking about the assignment (compare this to the *zea mays* essay in Chapter 5). If not, that might be even more interesting—a change of heart, an experience of growth and reflection.

6. Think of something you used to believe and don't believe anymore, something you thought was true but turned out to be false—write a few sentences about before and after and what caused the change. Does this seem to reflect your thoughtfulness and curiosity?

Finally, remember colleges are interested in your mind more than your biography. What has happened to you doesn't matter much. What matters is what you've thought about what has happened to you. Don't focus on event. Think of what your application won't show about your mind and your heart if it's just grades and numbers; then try to find an event that will illuminate that mind and that heart.

Chapter 6

Parents and the Process

Going to college is a family affair. The student is the main character, but all the family members—and all the family finances—take a supporting role. Parents advise, assist, and begin to imagine a smaller household. Siblings enjoy the shift of attention but also miss the older (and wiser?) brother or sister. Everyone says, "Thank goodness for e-mail." And the dog wonders why no one is sleeping in Junior's bed.

College selection, then, is collaboration. And it is probably the first family collaboration in which the child has a greater say than the parents. This chapter, therefore, offers some advice to parents as their children complete applications and write essays. It is meant to normalize the shocks and surprises, challenges and changes of this complicated and exciting moment. And although the rest of this book makes clear what role the applicant needs to take, this section addresses assignments for parents and guardians, *particularly those related to essay writing time*. Parents, regardless of their own educational experiences, can provide significant support for their children when it comes time to "Tell us about yourself."

In 2000-01, in research conducted for the National Association for College Admission Counseling, I asked seniors about their essay composition processes. The range of resources students turned to for help surprised me. Nearly every respondent acknowledged some kind of assistance in the process. But the guidance counselor didn't rank first. *Parents were the most significant source of help.* Even students living away at boarding schools said their parents had helped them at essay time. Teachers, especially English teachers, were cited, as were guidance counselors, educational consultants, and friends. But the results suggested that parents, who know the lives and personalities of their children, can help a son or daughter think about the topics and sift through their options. Duke University's application notes, "All good writers seek feedback, advice, or editing." Parents are uniquely situated to offer these things.

A Letter to Parents

In the college search, parents and their children talk, reflect, share, think, argue, and come to terms with change. There's value in the process as well as in the outcome. So a good first step, before any writing or talking begins, is to look into your own life and consider your expectations and assumptions. Zina Jacques, a former dean of admission and a director of a counseling center in Boston, notes: "The young people I work with apply to at least two colleges: the one their parents went to and the one their parents were rejected by." Whether you went to college or not, you have hopes for your children and, in particular, hopes that they will be even more successful than you were. So consider what you want for your child, separate that from what you want for yourself, and adjust your goals according to what's best for your son or daughter as a learner, as a young adult, "as is."

Timing

The calendar for parents mimics the one provided for students in Chapter 1. The junior year is a time of talk and gentle exploration. Conversations about options and reflections on your child as a learner are useful. There will be some testing that year and a little deflected stress as senior friends go through the search. But it's too early to set the sights or to eliminate anything; so much is still to be determined (grades, scores, captain of debate? conference champs?). For the same reasons, it's too early to start writing.

In the spring, you might visit a few campuses as your junior begins to receive school mailings. This is the time to search. Senior fall is the time of focus—a list of colleges is finalized, with help from the guidance counselor, and applications are completed, perhaps one in October, but most before the semester break. Winter, as for bears, is for hibernation. Another flurry of activity comes with early spring. Students hear from the colleges in March and April and choose by May 1. There will be confusions, delights, and disappointments. Ideally, several colleges your senior chose will choose her. The summer will include one trip to a giant store called something like Bed, Bath and Futon, and then several moments designed to make home a place she's willing to leave. ("Well, okay, but remember two months from now I'll be able to stay out all night if I want to." "While you're living in our house, young lady...." You get the idea.) Then they're gone and it's very quiet. This is a new phase, the right next thing, something you've worked for: less laundry, more e-mail, joy, confusion, adventure, change. You will remember that Mark Twain wasn't kidding when he said, "Youth is wasted on the young."

What You Can't Do

Before the "to-do" list, let's consider the "can't-do" list. Perhaps it will be liberating to consider what's not in your control and what's not expected of you.

- You can't make the high school guidance office into your own personal support system. Guidance is happy to help you ... and all the other senior families. If you do receive a significant amount of assistance, thank-you notes (or a plant for the guidance secretary) are appropriate. Teachers who write recommendations also prefer to receive forms with stamped envelopes, plenty of lead-time, and a follow-up thank you.

- You can't take the standardized tests or write your child's essay. Sharpened pencils, an apple, and new batteries for the calculator on test day are the limits of your power. (Tips on the right level of intervention at essay-writing time follow.)

- You can't change your child's decision style or fully protect him from the bumps and abrasions of this very public sorting. Someone will seem to do better without clear merit. Someone will say something cruel. Rejection is never easy. And Susan Tree, director of college counseling at the Westtown School, in Westtown, Pennsylvania, advises, "The process, done correctly, will have rejection in it somewhere."

- You can't let inertia teach its lesson here. It's easy to say, "Well, if he doesn't get his act together, he'll learn there won't be any choices left." Great for prom tickets or graduation gowns, but not appropriate for the college selection process. Kids are already conflicted and confused about this moment of judgment. They want to leave and they want to stay. They love you and they need to leave. As Diane Anci, dean of admission at Mount Holyoke, says, "They feel like a twig in the river. They ought to be the river." So don't complicate the matter by letting their irresponsibility bring them down. Let life do that later. Be helpful, inspire action, and get to the end as friends.

What You Can Do

You can frame conversations about college selection and the essay. Choose times when no one can distract them. Ask them to think about themselves as learners. *What classes have they loved? Hated? What teacher was a favorite? A nemesis? Do they like to talk in class? Do they work if no one's checking? Shine in essays and tests, or in comments and arguments in class? In college, will they still want to act, play the violin, play baseball, or run a model United Nations? A bunch of roommates or a single room? Big classes? Group work? Lectures? Vegan menu options? A cappella music groups? An adjacent city or a remote, silent wilderness?* By talking about the options in the future and the educational experiences in the past, you can help your senior look beyond name brands and think about the match of themselves and specific institutions. In this way, together, you begin building a prototype, i.e., a generic, ideal college template that can be plugged in at a variety of levels of competitiveness and selectivity.

Here's an example: I conclude that I am happiest in small, seminar classes and that the restrictions of a core curriculum are less appealing to me than the ability to choose courses according to my own interests. I am looking into environmental science, but I want a school where I can create my own major in the intersection of this discipline and government policy. I want a coed school, and I don't want fraternities to drive the social scene. I want my teachers to know me and the campus to be four to five blocks, not a zip code of its own. I don't want to be more than a three-to-four hour drive from home. Now, I can generate a list of six to eight schools (nationwide, there are 3,000 schools to choose among) that fit the criteria but represent a range of selectivity from the very selective (less than 20 percent of applicants are admitted), through selective (20–40 percent are admitted), to less selective (greater than 40 percent are admitted). If I can create a clear definition of my perfect school and if all my applications go to schools that fit the prototype, I will get what I want wherever I enroll. (As the parent and chief financial officer in this collaboration, remember to identify any absolutes in the process—if it can't be on the other side of the country or cost more than $10,000, say so early.)

The Essay

Most important, you can talk about the application essay with your senior. And the emphasis here is on the word "talk." *But not about the essay questions.* The essay is meant to be an additional lens on the applicant, a source of information beyond the scores, grades, and activities list. It is included so that colleges can evaluate the applicant's writing ability and also uncover a sense of the applicant's ideas, values, and point of view. The questions all come down to the same thing: Tell us about yourself. Your role is to help the child look at that "yourself" and decide what's worth telling. You both have 17 years of information to share; you have the maturity of age to temper the process.

So begin with a conversation about your child's strengths and positive attributes. Tell them what you think they're very good at, your favorite personality features, or a habit of thinking or acting you appreciate. Go for adjectives, not nouns. Talk about what you love about them, what others have said, what comes up in teacher conferences or shines forth in their performances, games, kitchen conversations, or family interactions. A list of first-round thoughts might be: hardworking, committed, enthusiastic, optimistic, energetic, smart, cheerful, willing to help. Or maybe your offspring is creative, spontaneous, generous, innovative, individualistic, reflective, sensitive, adaptable. These lists represent two different people—your green-haired daughter? Your sweet C+ son?—but each has strengths.

As an adviser, recast discouragement as hope. If they say, "I don't know what I want to study," you can offer, "That's neat…you're clearly interested in everything!" Not only are you supplying a possible focus for the essay; this conversation is much-needed praise and affection at a time when the world seems rather dark and judgmental.

Your son or daughter may be unwilling to play along with this game. If they don't want your input, you can provide a sympathetic listening ear, asking about their plans to date. Best not to ask about what other people are doing—that feels like criticism. If you are afraid they are heading in the wrong direction, find a guidance counselor, teacher, coach, godmother, or paid educational consultant to join the process. Experienced and credentialed independent educational consultants can be found through the Independent Educational Consultants Association in Fairfax, Virginia (www.ieca-online.com). When a son or daughter refuses help, it is, of course, a sign of emerging independence (this never seems to apply to the ironing or car insurance). But your senior does need someone as a sounding board. It's easy to get off-track answering any high-stakes question; this is not the time to "go it alone" entirely. Conversely, it's also easy to be intimidated and waste the opportunity with something safe, predictable, and utterly forgettable. An English teacher, a coach, or a guidance counselor can help. Because of their limited experience, friends are a last resort. But "it takes a village to write an essay," says Brad MacGowan, an educational researcher and veteran counselor at Newton North High School, in Newton, Massachusetts. For MacGowan, every writer needs "reciprocal contact with knowledgeable adults." So if discourse doesn't happen at your dinner table, encourage your senior to find it on the field or in the classroom.

If, however, the conversation leads to notes on the back of a fast-food napkin, you've got an idea bank. Look it over. Eliminate things revealed by the rest of the application. "Smart" may be adequately addressed by the transcript. "Athletic" will be there in the MVP award. "Involved" will be obvious from the activities list. Then ask what major strength or characteristic of your child is missing from the application. With only the transcript and scores, will admissions know about his drive, his humor, his generous spirit, his creativity, his analytic and inquisitive way of thinking? Can the essay fill in the blanks?

Now list some events, stories, or "hot spot" moments that make evident the missing characteristic. Be sure to focus on the characteristic, not the event that reveals it. Choose a story tailored to your theme: creativity (as seen through an alternate assignment developed for 10th-grade science) or insight (as seen though the experience of winning/losing a class election) or stamina and loyalty (as seen through four years of losing field hockey teams). The topic should be the creativity, the insight, or the commitment. The wind tunnel, the race for class president, life as a goalie: use it as an illumination of character and personality.

Together, you're a team of experts that can bring both positive energy and a sense of good judgment to the planning. But don't dictate a topic. Even if your senior chooses a weak idea to begin with (and this is the normal pattern), since you're planning a *list* of possibilities here, there will be an idea bank of options to return to if Plan A turns into Plan B. Regardless of your educational background, first language, income, or achievements, you can help in the essay planning.

Batting around ideas and possibilities is fair game for anyone with an interest in the young person…but once the writing begins, you belong on the sidelines. Read Chapters 3, 4, and 5 of this book for a fuller sense of how the writer will proceed after your involvement. But leave the red pencil in your desk and stick with "discourse" as the best way to be helpful.

Final Tips

- Schedule time to generate a preliminary idea bank for the essay, brainstorming together once in the junior-year spring and then again in the senior-year fall. It will serve as a useful resource as the business of applying gets serious. And it has extra benefits. Students need to do some self-examination in order to make wise choices in college; this kind of thinking and talking can enrich every aspect of the application, even the interview.

- Talk, don't write. Be active when ideas are flying around, and avoid hands-on editing. Once the ideas are out there, the student should own the rest of the writing process. You might proofread for typos. But a teacher or a guidance counselor may be a more familiar (and less painful) source of gentle suggestion and light editing (grammatical and usage errors, spots of confusion, school-specific jargon). Stick to talking about the essay. Don't spoil the spontaneity or change the style of the essay. My experience with hands-on parent editing is that it usually turns a good kid essay into a mediocre lawyer essay.

- Be true to your child. Don't encourage your senior to write about an imagined topic meant to please admission personnel. There is no such thing. You cannot predict who will read an application— the dean with 30 years experience (he loves cross-country skiing, murder mysteries with culinary subplots, and syndicated episodes of M*A*S*H), or the new hire who graduated last May (she loves spinning, Nora Roberts, and *The Bachelorette*). Instead, focus on what admissions needs to know about this applicant. Forget "What should I say?" and ask, "What don't they know?"

- Don't despair if you aren't a big part of this collaboration at the beginning. Students do care what their parents think, and you will be important in the final decision, even if you're a sideline adviser along the way. Be ready for soul-searching conversations in April as students make their final decisions and discover that they actually have to leave home and attend one of these places.

Conclusion

Regardless of your knowledge of colleges or your own education achievements, you are an expert on your child. You are therefore an important helper in the collaboration called applying to college. Together, you and your senior can work out the right degree of involvement for everyone. Tell your senior you won't nag if he will create a checklist of chores and deadlines and post it on the refrigerator door. Together, access help from the high school where, alas, your deadlines are everyone else's deadlines. Or get help from admission offices (I promise the admission secretary does *not* keep a log in which to note "Parent of Thomas Smith called—asked a silly question"). Recognize those tasks that are entirely your responsibility, like the necessary tax forms for financial aid applications. Then do your homework and keep your ears and options open. Most important, provide encouragement and assure your son or daughter that the process, in general, is fair, supported by helpful professionals, and neither the last nor the only decision they will make about their education and their future. If things go wrong, most mistakes can be corrected (transfer? year off? guest semester?).

At essay-writing time, remind students that:

- they've written essays before; they have the necessary writing skills

- they know (and love) this topic—themselves

- the essay isn't the only factor in the admissions decision (if they work hard, it has the potential to be a positive factor)

- there are helpers to turn to

- this is a chance to shine if they can write solid prose of memorable insight

Pam Reynolds, an educational consultant based in Needham, Massachusetts, likes to say, "I loved being a mom. I hated being a parent." This is one time, however, when being a parent is more rewarding than the rule-making and lecture life of the preschool years. Parents are incredibly important to their daughters and sons as the family dynamic changes and children head off to complete their educations. With patience on both sides, the process—and even the essay—can be a successful collaboration.

Quick Fixes to Make the Essay Work for Your Child

"*Show—don't tell*": good advice for writers, and an adage you can help your son or daughter put to work. Conversations at the dinner table will help them find a subject that adds to their application and illuminates their life. Even more useful will be some later conversations about what they've thought about this subject and how they have acted upon those thoughts. A new version of the adage could be "*Not what you've done—what you've thought about what you've done.*"

In this paragraph, the applicant was asked to write about an activity that had special meaning for him. He wrote about his athletic career in high school. The first part of the paragraph doesn't do much more than name his sports involvements and remind the reader that, besides the games, there were plenty of practices and conditioning sessions involved. However, as he begins to think about the hours he spent, we see something of his reflective habit of mind. And in the second team citation and the tough loss to an old rival, we get information that goes beyond what's on the transcript and in the rest of the application: the author reveals himself to be dedicated, satisfied with hard effort when victory proves elusive, and able to find enduring friendships in the locker-room relationships.

This section of the paragraph describes activities that probably can be intuited from the application.

Here the applicant has added material that is not duplicated elsewhere in the application and that demonstrates his values and style of thinking.

Two and a half hours a day, six days a week, nine months a year, for four years. Forgetting travel time, or freshman football, or the summer training, or the miles of running and hours of lifting for wrestling and football and lacrosse, 12 varsity letters has meant about 2100 hours in my high school career. I often wonder what I would have done with all that time if I hadn't played sports. I could have done homework, I suppose, or gotten a few extra hours of sleep each night. But then, I imagine life wouldn't mean quite as much to me. In football, I was awarded the second team all-league for outside linebackers this year. It's just a piece of paper to everyone else—a smile and a "congratulations." But to me, it's up-downs in the mud after practice; it's the fourth-quarter against BHS when I can't walk but I can still run; it's driving the tackle sled until I wish I never played this sport; and it's tears in the locker room with the 25 guys I knew best who gave it everything and still fell seven points short to BHS. It's been 17 years since we've beaten them and we were seven points away. No one else will remember this year's score either; I'll remember how close we came and the 2100 hours.

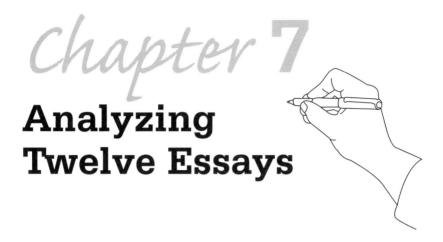

Chapter 7

Analyzing Twelve Essays

The 12 sample essays that follow demonstrate a variety of strengths and weaknesses. None is presented as a perfect or "correct" college essay. Marilyn McGrath Lewis, director of admission at Harvard, says the essay is "a very important part of the application, and in some ways the most personal part." Thus for admissions personnel, "there is no one standard." These samples are meant to suggest the breadth of options you have in introducing yourself to a college.

Sample 1

I guess it was inevitable that I'd be on hockey skates at some point in my life, but I did not expect that I'd become one of a rare group of female ice hockey officials before I even reached high school. Being born into a family of hockey players and figure skaters, it seemed that my destiny had already been decided.

Right from the beginning, my two older brothers and my father strapped me up and threw me onto the ice. I loved it and, in my mind, I was on my way to becoming a female Gretzky! But my mom had to think of something fast to drag her little girl away from this sport of ruffians. Enter my first hot pink figure skating dress! That was all it took to launch fifteen years of competitive figure skating. Even though figure skating soon became my passion, I always had an unsatisfied yearning for ice hockey. It took a great deal of convincing from my parents that competitive figure skating and ice hockey didn't mix.

My compromise became refereeing ice hockey; little did I know that I was beginning an activity that would influence my character and who I am today. When I began, I would only work with my dad and brothers. Everyone was friendly and accepting because I had just started. I soon realized though that to get better I needed to start refereeing with people I wasn't related to, and that's when my experience drastically changed. An apologetic smile and an "I'm sorry" wasn't going to get me through games now. As I began officiating higher-level games and dealing with more arrogant coaches, I suddenly entered a new male-dominated world, a world I had never experienced before. My confidence was shot, and all I wanted to do was get through each game and be able to leave. Sometimes I was even too scared to skate along the teams' benches because I would get upset by what the coaches would yell to me. "Do you have a hot date tonight, ref?" was a typical comment that coaches would spit at me during the course of a game. In their eyes, I did not belong on that ice, and they were going to do whatever they could do to make sure no women wanted to officiate their games. I was determined not to let them chase me off the ice.

I made the decision to stand up for myself. I never responded rudely to the coaches, but I did not let them walk all over me and destroy my confidence anymore. I started to act and feel more like the 4-year certified Atlantic District Official that I am. There were still a few situations that scared me. One time I called a penalty in a championship game during the third overtime and the team I penalized ended up losing because they got scored on. I knew I had made the right call, even though I was unnerved when I saw the losing teams' parents waiting for me at my locker room; for the moment I wished I hadn't called that penalty. Although it was scary at the time, I stood my ground and overcame my fears. That was an important stepping-stone in my officiating career and in my life.

After four years of refereeing, I still can't say it's easy. Every game hands me something new and I never know what to expect. Now I have the confidence and preparation to deal with the unexpected, on and off the ice. I now also know to take everything with a grain of salt and not let it get to me. I have learned that life is just like being out on the ice; if I am prepared and act with confidence, I will be perceived as confident. These are the little lessons that I'm grateful to have learned as a woman referee.

Things to Notice About This Essay

1. The author tells an interesting story about her experiences as a referee.
2. A sense of her personality—determination, flexibility, good humor—comes through in the narration.
3. Details like "Do you have a hot date tonight, ref?" make the narration memorable (we'd love to hear more of these kinds of details).
4. The essay needs a faster start. The first paragraph (three sentences) says the same thing in both the first and third sentences—and gives away the essay's surprise in the second! A good revision would delete all of paragraph one and start at paragraph two.
5. There's too much frame here and not enough picture. The essay needs further development, especially about the difficulties of becoming and being a ref, to keep it vivid.
6. The author should "dwell" in the meaning of the experience a little more at the end—"I wonder about...I also think...Sometimes I believe...." Significant experiences like this one, woven through many years of the author's life, don't mean just one thing—there are more insights and lessons to explore here.

Sample 2

From the time I was able to realize what a university was, all I heard from my mother's side of the family was about the University of Michigan and the great heritage it has. Many a Saturday afternoon my grandfather would devote to me, by sitting me down in front of the television and reminiscing about the University of Michigan while halftime occurred during a Michigan Wolverines football game. Later, as I grew older and universities took on greater meaning, my mother and uncle, both alumni of the University of Michigan, took me to see their old stamping grounds. From first sight, the university looked frightening because of its size, but with such a large school comes diversity of people and of academic and non-academic events.

In Springfield High School, non-academic clubs such as the Future Physicians and the Pylon, both of which I have belonged to for two years, give me an opportunity to see both the business world and the medical world. These two clubs have given me a greater sense of what these careers may be like. In Future Physicians, I participated in field trips to children's hospitals and also participated in two bloodbanks.

Currently I hold a job at Maas Brothers. This lets me interact with people outside my own immediate environment. I meet different kinds of people, in different moods, with different attitudes, and with different values. This job teaches me to be patient with people, to have responsibility, and to appreciate people for what they are.

In the community I am active in my church Youth Group. As a high school sophomore, I was our church's representative to the Diocesan Youth Fellowship. I helped organize youth group events, the largest being "The Bishop's Ball," a state-wide event for 300 young people. I also played high school junior varsity soccer for two years. As a senior I will be playing varsity soccer, but in the off-season. As a junior I coached a girls' soccer team for the town. This gave me a great deal of responsibility, because the care of twenty-four girls was put into my custody. It felt very satisfying to pass on the knowledge of soccer to another generation. The girls played teams from other parts of Florida. Though their record was 3-8, the girls enjoyed their season. This is what I taught them was the greatest joy of soccer.

The past three years of my life have given me greater visions of my future. I see the University of Michigan as holding a large book with many unread chapters and myself as an eager child who has just learned to read. I intend to read and probe into all the chapters. The University of Michigan offers me more than the great reputation of this fine school, but a large student body with diverse likes and dislikes, and many activities, both academic and non-academic, to participate in. With the help of the University of Michigan, I will be successful after college and be able to make a name and place for myself in our society.

Things to Notice About This Essay

1. It follows a general essay organization, with an introduction, several body paragraphs about different activities, and a conclusion that returns to the earlier idea of Michigan's diversity.
2. It has no focus but rather jumps around from the school to the writer and from point to point. Notice especially the lack of transition from the first paragraph to the second: how did we get from Michigan's diversity to the writer's clubs?
3. The body paragraphs lack *proof*: What are these clubs and jobs, what did he do in each one, how many field trips were taken, and what was his role?
4. What's Pylon? What does he do at Maas Brothers?
5. There are plenty of generalizations but no evidence to back up any of them. How did these activities give him a greater sense of the career

world? "Participated" and "interact" are pretty vague words. Compare the discussion of Maas Brothers with the hockey ref's story.

6. There is very little specific knowledge of what the University of Michigan has to offer.

7. The style is rather stuffy and awkward ("while halftime occurred," "the care of twenty-four girls was put into my custody").

8. Most important, nearly everything described here appears elsewhere on the application, under sports, jobs, extracurricular activities, and alumni connections.

9. The writer would be well advised to focus on *one* of the things discussed in this essay. Perhaps he could show the reader his work with the girls' soccer team. What he did to make Jennifer and Gretchen and Courtney enjoy soccer even though they only won three of their games would be more vivid than a lot of talk about passing things on to future generations.

10. In short, the essay seems full of information and displays adequate form, but it lacks *focus* and *proof.*

Sample 3

My most important experience sought me out. It happened to me; I didn't cause it.

My preferred companions are books or music or pen and paper. I have only a small circle of close friends, few of whom get along together. They could easily be counted "misfits." To be plain, I found it quite easy to doubt my ability to have any sort of "close relationship."

After the closing festivities of Andover Summer School this past summer, on the night before we were scheduled to leave, a girl I had met during the program's course approached me. She came to my room and sat down on my bed and announced that she was debating with herself whether she wanted me to become her boyfriend. She wanted my reaction, my opinion.

I was startled, to say the least, and frightened. I instantly said, "No." I told her I on no account wanted this and that I would reject any gestures she made towards starting a relationship. I would ignore her entirely, if need be. I explained that I was a coward. I wanted nothing whatsoever to do with a relationship. I talked a lot and very fast.

To my surprise, she did not leave instantly. Instead, she hugged her knees and rocked back and forth on my bed. I watched her from across the room. She rocked, and I watched. Doubts crept up on me. Opportunity had knocked and the door was still locked. It might soon depart.

"I lied," I said. "I was afraid of what might happen if we became involved. But it's better to take the chance than to be afraid."

She told me she knew I had lied. I had made her realize, though, how much she actually wanted me to be her boyfriend. We decided to keep up a relationship after Andover.

Even then, I was not sure which had been the lie. Now I think that everything I said may have been true when I said it. But I'm still not sure.

I learned, that night, that I could be close to someone. I also realize, now, that it doesn't matter whether or not that person is a misfit; the only important thing is the feeling, the closeness, the connection. As long as there is something between two people—friendship, love, shared interests, whatever else—it is a sign that there can be some reconciliation with fear, some "fit" for misfits. And it shows that fear need not always win, that we can grow and change, and even have second chances.

I am still seeing her.

Things to Notice About This Essay

1. It follows the standard essay pattern: an introduction (short), a series of supporting paragraphs for the body, and a conclusion (here, a summary paragraph and an end sentence).
2. It has a *focus*: his anxiety about relationships.
3. It has *proof*: the story of his conversation with a girl. Again, focused narrative development has made the proof vivid.
4. It is short, to the point, simple, and yet memorable. It is interesting without being grand, noble, or cosmic.
5. The style is simple and direct, employing short sentences and simple words to tell a simple story.
6. It coordinates and enriches an application full of academic achievements and high scores and grades. It is information definitely not found elsewhere in the application.

Sample 4

My childhood left three months ago on a plane to Austria.

It was a sad day, the end of June, when my baby cousins moved away. They had lived nearby for almost five years, and now they were moving to a country too far to visit with any regularity. My cousins were a fundamental part of my life; when they were not with me, they were on my mind. A week had never gone by without a visit from them and I doubted my life would be the same without them. They brought back the untroubled days of my childhood, through games, adventures, and silliness; and yet they helped mature me from an at-times selfish teenager into a responsible, mature adult.

My aunt and uncle moved to New Jersey from Boston, with their 1-year-old daughter Yasmeen, in the winter of 1998. They lived in an apartment on the side of our house and I was ecstatic to have our family, especially a baby girl, so close to us. Yasmeen had close friendships with each of my sisters, but

I knew the one that developed between us was the strongest. As she began to walk on her own and talk in full sentences, I realized the extent of my influence upon her. I would notice her syntax and mannerisms mimicking mine. I also noticed when she'd copy some of my more unpleasant actions, arguing with her mother after I had done the same. Yasmeen made me realize what being a role model really was.

When Maya was born in 2000, Yasmeen had a hard time adjusting. She was jealous of the attention we all paid to her new younger sister, so I did my best to pay attention to her when she might have not been noticed. Once Yasmeen overcame her jealousy, she was able to enjoy Maya's presence in our lives, like we all did. Maya grew up fast, too, it seemed. Each day, they got a little bit bigger, and I tried to take advantage of our times together, doing my best to free my schedule for my two favorite people.

My experience with Yasmeen and Maya has brought me to realize the importance of influential people. I know that I have helped Yasmeen and Maya grow, but "the babies" have made an even great impact on my own life. They have shown me how to be a parent, a sister, a cousin, a babysitter, a child, and most importantly, a friend. My relationship with my cousins has made me a better person—a more patient person, with the ability to tolerate endless questions and spilled juice; an exuberant person, able to have fun and be happy with others and sometimes, when I'd rather not, for the sake of others; a role model, showing the babies the ethics of life, right, wrong, and in between; and a compassionate person, able to be responsible, forgiving, and loving. Yasmeen and Maya made me know that I can and do affect people's lives and emotions. They are where I leave a lasting impression. And maybe, as they grow, they won't remember all the fun times we had, but I do know they'll remember the things I tried to teach them about life and love and family.

Things to Notice About This Essay

1. The essay has a sharp, strong beginning and a fresh honesty that conveys the events of the author's life and her outlook.
2. The style is simple and the topic is, too. But we believe in this story because of its simplicity.
3. The author proves that this has been a significant experience by the lessons she enumerates in the last paragraph.
4. The reader needs to know a little more about the circumstances of these moves from Boston to New Jersey to Austria, in order to understand the context of the essay.
5. A few more specific examples in the second and third paragraphs would give them the same strength and vividness as the "spilled juice" reference.
6. Having shared this interesting story, the author might find a few more insights and results to add to the last paragraph. The events seem affecting; the effects might be multiplied.

Sample 5

It has come to my attention that our nation, and nations like ours, have long been plagued by a mysterious occurrence. An occurrence that is as perplexing as it is frustrating, and as baffling as it is widespread, a problem that finds its origins at the very foot of our society. The problem of which I speak is none other than "The Orphan Sock Enigma," the constant disappearance of individual socks during the laundering process. It is a problem familiar to all of us, and also one to which we have unwillingly admitted defeat [sic].

I recently decided that this puzzle had remained unsolved for too long, and resolved to find an explanation. (In the grand tradition of science, I refused to be discouraged by the basic irrelevance of my cause.) But the truth that I uncovered is more shocking and fantastic than I could have ever imagined.

My procedures, observations, and conclusions are as follows:

First, to verify that the problem exists, experimental and control loads of laundry were completely processed (put through the washer and dryer). In the experimental load (load with socks), by the end of the process, some socks were lost. But in the control load (load without socks), no socks were lost. Thus, the problem was verified.

Next the progress of a load of socks was carefully monitored. The results indicated that sock disappearance occurs during the period of time when the load is in the dryer. Following this conclusion, a literature search was done and a very significant fact was uncovered: there is no mention of socks disappearing in dryers before the invention of dryers in the 1920s. All evidence clearly pointed to the dryer. And it is there that I would find the answer to the enigma.

Then, the actual experiment was done. In four separate trials, a number of socks (ten socks, or five pairs) were put through a normal drying cycle. The types of socks tested were selected by the highly accurate Harvey-Allman Principle Hierarchy and Zero Alternative Reduction Dimension (HAP-HAZARD).

TRIAL #	#1	#2	#3	#4
Initial Mass 10 socks	265g	270g	276g	261g
Final Mass remaining socks and lint	261g	266g	271g	256g
Temp. running, empty dryer	65.56°C	65.56°C	65.56°C	65.56°C
Temp. running, dryer with socks	70.56°C	70.56°C	71.56°C	71.56°C
Net change in mass	4.0g	4.0g	5.0g	5.0g
Net change in temp.	5.0°C	5.0°C	6.25°C	6.25°C

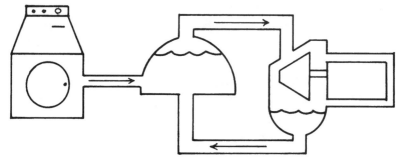

Fig. 1. Simplified Diagram of a "Sock Reactor."

The mass of the total load was measured prior to processing. Upon completion of the cycle, the mass of the remaining load plus the lint collected was also measured. In addition, the temperature of a running, empty dryer was measured, as was the temperature of a running, full dryer during the cycle. A table of data follows.

In each and every trial, one or two of the socks were lost (each from a different pair). More importantly, in each and every trial, there was a net loss of mass and also a net increase in temperature. These results suggested a test hypothesis. Through the use of Einstein's equation for mass-energy equivalence, $E=mc^2$, the net loss of mass was completely and totally accounted for by the net increase in temperature. All the evidence clearly pointed to one unavoidable, momentous conclusion: all the socks that had been disappearing in countries all over the world had been directly converted to energy (or that there was something seriously wrong with my dryer). I have just begun to realize the monumental importance and far-reaching implications of my discovery. Quite possibly, it could completely change the way we live our lives (and do our laundry) for years to come.

From further experimentation, it seems that the amount of energy liberated (and mass lost) is directly related to the amount of the fiber Spandex in the sock.

But for some reason, the Spandex must be in the form of a sock for the reaction to take place. Therefore, by increasing the amount of Spandex in a sock, one can increase the amount of energy liberated. It also seems that the reaction can be controlled by the presence of different numbers of fabric softening sheets, similar to the effect of control rods in a nuclear reactor. In light of these discoveries, my house is now completely powered by a "Sock Reactor."

I estimate that just a few "Sock Reactors" could supply power to a city the size of Chicago with zero danger (provided a good supply of fabric softening sheets is on hand). This is because one hundred percent of the mass is completely converted into energy safely, easily, and without leaving any of that unsightly radioactive waste common to those other name brand reactors. Therefore, you and your loved ones are spared from that embarrassing radiation sickness and unpleasant aftertaste.

Originally, I had hoped to keep knowledge of this discovery fairly restricted, but I fear that word has leaked out. I have reason to believe there is a merger planned between Interwoven Hosiery and General Power's nuclear division.

Although I have not been able to explain why only one sock out of a pair can be converted, it appears to in some way relate to a black hole, a time warp, and static cling.

Albert Einstein, the man who first discovered the mass-energy equivalence, never wore socks. I think that just about says it all.

Things to Notice About This Essay

1. It's written in essay form. It has an introduction, several paragraphs of proof, and a clear conclusion. However, it's also a creative piece that is not easily translatable into formulas or patterns.
2. It has a *focus*: the "Orphan Sock Enigma."
3. It is specific: the problem, the research, the chart and figure make

it real and vivid. The author clearly knows how to plan, run, and record a scientific study, as well as how to spoof one.

4. This is a production piece that few seniors could do. However, if you can write with comparable flair and humor, it is a reasonable option for a college essay. It presents a good picture of the writer, his interest in science, his imagination and humor, how extensively he thinks about life, and how well he can write.

Sample 6

"I'm so bad at this," she said, shaking her red-orange hair. Michaela was standing in the middle of the soccer field holding a ball in her hands. She was trying to juggle it off her thighs, but couldn't do it more than three times in a row.

"No, you're not," I said. "Lots of the other kids are having trouble too."

She shook her head again. Without even noticing the other kids scattering after their balls as if they were trying to capture little runaway pets, she stuck out her bottom lip.

"Listen Michaela," I said, "When I was your age, I couldn't even juggle the soccer ball, let alone juggle it three times."

"But you can juggle it like a thousand times now, and I can't even get to four. It's not fair," she said.

Michaela pounded her soccer ball onto the ground and sat down on it. Her elbows rested on her knees and her chin came down on her fists. I sat down next to her.

"Michaela, how old are you?'

"Ten," she said jutting her chin out slightly.

"Do you know how old I am?"

"No."

"I'm seventeen. I've had seven years to practice my juggling and to get better at it. That's all it takes, practice. All you have to do is try to juggle the ball five times every day, and more when you can do that. Eventually, you'll be able to juggle more than I can," I said, looking at her with conviction.

She was staring at the ground pulling tufts of grass up and piling little haystacks on top of her cleats. I could tell she wasn't sure whether to believe me or not. I got up and went to help some of the other kids, to give her a chance to think. Helping them seemed to mix encouragement in equal parts with leaving them alone with the challenge. One of the boys had given up altogether and was sitting on his soccer ball trying to peel an orange he'd kept from snacktime. Our coach called the kids around. Michaela got up and pouted her soccer ball up to the rest of the group. Matthew ran up to me on his way to the group and handed me his orange.

"Will you peel this for me?" he asked.

"Sure," I said.

I took the orange. The skin was slippery and slightly more yellow than orange. I thought about how hard it is to peel an orange. You have to dig your fingernail in far enough to get under the peel, but not so far as to puncture the flesh. Each piece is independent and seldom do you get a piece that makes the next one easier to peel. I poised the orange on my fingertips and tried to peel the first few pieces. Those are toughest; the skin is always the hardest and won't stay connected. I could feel bits of grainy peel under my fingernails. The kids started walking to lunch.

"Here you go," I said handing the orange back to Matthew, with a thick peel "pull tab" rising from the top. "I got it started, you should be able to take it from here."

Things to Notice About This Essay

1. The author chooses an appropriately focused topic: a brief moment, a short pair of conversations in a single day of summer work.
2. A sense of the writer's talents as a writer and as a teacher are clear from this story.
3. The strategy is subtle, leaving most of the conclusions to the reader.

4. The essay is very short, banking on the reader to get the point.
5. This essay uses a high-risk strategy. Will the reader conclude the author is coming to college to play soccer or to study child development? The author is counting on the story to carry the meaning and omits the "From this I have learned..." conclusion. It works, but just barely.

Sample 7

I used to be a pretty deep guy. I watched foreign films, read Nietzsche, and stayed up all night "contemplating jazz." I was Jack Kerouac living in a fire hut on top of Desolation Peak. I was Gary Snyder seeking enlightenment in a Buddhist monastery in Thailand. I was Ken Kesey, Jimi Hendrix, and Timothy Leary all rolled up in one gigantic mess of pseudo-intellectual, adolescent, fancy boarding school beat poet wannabe. I was a moron.

I blew off my schoolwork not because I was lazy, but because I thought that schoolwork was shallow, too insignificant for me, the vivacious intellectual, the dharma bum, the Zen lunatic wanderer. How could my teachers expect me to do their homework, when life around me was all so futile, so meaningless? I was sure that I was a tortured soul destined to lead a life full of angst and pain.

That was last fall, more than a year ago now. In February of last year, I left my hipster friends and their coffeehouse conversations behind, to move back to the suburbs of Philadelphia and my conservative, unhip public high school. Suburban Philadelphia is not the easiest place in the world to be sixties cool and stylish. There aren't many smoke-filled coffeehouses or hippie wanderers. It's clean here, upper middle class—you know, the Ford Explorer, Saturday evening Mass, country club for dinner scene. I came back to Philadelphia because it isn't all that "hip," because there is nothing "profound" to do. I came home to get myself together. It was time to grow up.

I'm not as cool as I used to be. I never do anything very exciting or off the wall, at least not by my old standards. My friends from boarding school have for the most part become nothing more than distant memories. They're all off in New York City or Mexico pretending to work on their spirituality, but really just partying their lives away. I stay home a lot. I'm at the library a couple of nights a week. I read, I write letters, I do some painting.

Last weekend, I watched *The Color Purple* with my mom, collected some weather data for a chemistry project, and had a tea party with my little sister. I've been spending time with the people I met in my high school production of *Arsenic and Old Lace*, too. I feel balanced; I feel like myself. I no longer want to tend bar in Tangiers or meditate in Sri Lanka . . . all right, maybe I do, but not right now. For so long, I wanted to be other people, to be a cultural icon, a legend in my own time. But in reality, I'm nothing like Keith Richards. Honestly, I'm a little scared of sex and drugs. I worry about pimples, whether my parents are still happily married, where I'm going to be next year.

I came home, I grew up, I got my life back together. I'm still trying to find a balance, but I no longer feel like a reckless child. I was sure that I could get away from myself by just pretending that I was someone else. But right now, I'm not looking to be "on the road." I'm pretty happy being right where I am.

Things to Notice About This Essay

1. The story this writer tells seems sincere. It explains things from his transcript: a change of schools, improving grades.
2. The essay expects the reader to know all the references here to people (Gary Snyder, Keith Richards) and literature (*On the Road, Dharma Bums,* the line from poet Allen Ginsberg about "contemplating jazz"). The writer has a real depth of knowledge, which is

good, but in some of these references, he may be expecting a little too much from the reader . . . who won't be 17.

3. The essay has a clear focus ("It was time to grow up"), extensive use of specifics and descriptive details, and a strong sense of a writer who has thought about his life experiences.

4. The essay doesn't follow a traditional organization pattern and there are a few liberties with word choice and spelling ("wannabe"). A bit of a "risk," this essay does match a writer who himself has taken chances. He tells *his* story with grace and conviction.

Sample 8

As a seventeen year old, I don't yet have the experience or vision to know exactly what I want to accomplish. What I hope college will do for me is to broaden my base of knowledge with a solid liberal arts education. I would like to have the power to explore Drake's equation for extraterrestrial life while at the same time analyzing the similes used in Virgil's *Aeneid*. Or maybe I could investigate the applications of integral calculus or the themes of self-sacrifice in Shakespeare. From the combination of courses I decide to take, I expect to find one or two true passions that I can extract from the rest and then expand my knowledge exponentially in that field.

While I am working towards an academic concentration, I would like to focus my athletic efforts on swimming. At Springfield High, my intense training in swimming is interrupted every winter by my commitment to the basketball team. I am confident that concentrating solely on swimming will enable me to improve my past performances and times. If I could post a University record at Blodgett Pool and also find those one or two academic passions, I will have attained what I wanted from Princeton. And I am hopeful that in combining and completing these goals, I will have given something back to the school.

Things to Notice About This Essay

1. The writer's use of specific topics from a liberal arts curriculum suggests that she has thought about what's going to go on in college (Drake, Virgil, calculus, Shakespeare). Weaker sentences are those lacking specifics (Sentence 2: "broaden my base of knowledge with a solid liberal arts education." Final sentence: "combining and completing these goals, I will have given something back to the school").
2. The writer is honest about her plans and her inability to predict a future at least four years away. But she is also positive about what she's isn't sure of, emphasizing the future possibilities rather than her indecision.
3. It's a good idea to show a familiarity with the buildings and programs of the school to which you're applying. But if you write several essays like this one, be sure to proofread carefully. Isn't Blodgett Pool at Harvard?

Sample 9

I knew I was going to Pittsburgh to play in a tournament. I didn't know I would be visiting Houston, Pennsylvania between matches. A rural suburb twenty miles outside the city's industrial hub, Houston is my father's hometown.

His family, he says, was "dirt poor" and barely able to sustain the house we found still standing—tired of living, it seemed, and shedding its blue paint. My father pointed to a street corner blanketed with scattered sections of a local paper: "It was there . . . right there . . . where I stood and looked around me and saw that my future was contained in this town. It was painful to think of leaving. That street corner was the center of my universe." My father was the first person in his family—the first person in the little mining town—to go to college.

As my father drove me along the unpaved back roads, he tried to find messages and axioms in the half-century old tale, but they did not answer the chain of questions jerked along by my consciousness: *How did he get out? Why did he come back? Why did he want to bring me here? Can I be as proud of my life as he is of his? What do I have to accomplish to gain such satisfaction? Do I have to do it soon?*

His stories stacked on top of each other likes books on a desk. Each anecdote was another volume from his childhood and I was struggling to keep up with the reading. We passed the old house six times before he was ready to separate himself from Houston this time. The children playing outside the house tried to examine us through the tinted glass of our rented car and I shifted uncomfortably in my bucket seat. What opportunities did they have? What would I do with mine?

"Dad, these people are going to call the police if we keep circling the block."

Back at our hotel in Pittsburgh, I shouldered my racquet bag and followed my father up the staircase to our room. On each step, I tried to plant my foot exactly where he had put his.

Things to Notice About This Essay

1. The organization is basically narrative. The writer's insights and reflections are incorporated into the story of her visit to Houston, Pennsylvania.
2. The writer does not tell the reader what this experience means. It's a risk, but she assumes we will figure out the connection between her father's experiences and her own. The italicized section in the middle guides the reader in understanding the end.
3. The writer supplies the details needed to create a picture of the place. The use of realistic dialogue adds credibility.
4. The essay tells only a small story, but it reveals the writer's ability both to think about her own experiences and to understand the experiences of other, different people.

Sample 10

Finding Nemo is playing every hour on the hour this week. The theater teems with ornery, hyperactive kids for the half hour before each show. We have thirty minutes between each surge to sweep the floors of the concession stand before the next wave arrives to plead with their parents for four-dollar plastic buckets of junk food.

For $4.75 an hour after taxes (a little more than one of those buckets costs), it isn't the best summer job and it only feels like the worst when *Finding Nemo* is playing. Usually we have plenty of time between shows to sweep up popcorn and replenish cups, buckets, and lids from the strangely-shaped cupboards underneath the counter where you have to grope blindly while on your knees. It's even more exciting when looking for the vats of simulated butter, which leave ominous oil-and-artificial-flavoring cakes on the bottom of the shelves. I used to order "butter topping" with my movie popcorn. After one day of pouring vats of it into the heating and dispensing machine, I decided I could never order it again.

I wish I could say it has been an educational experience, that it has made me a better person, or that for whatever reason I am secretly Forrest Gump. But the truth is that I spent the summer in an air conditioned theater with free movies to earn enough money to pay for gas. And during the summer, that's all that matters in a teenager's world.

Things to Notice About This Essay

1. Asked to write about his summer activities, this writer tells the truth about his job in a clever and entertaining way.
2. There is no great lesson being taught but still the essay offers a clear focus—what he did last summer—and specifics that make that experience vivid and memorable to the reader.

3. The writer uses irony in the contrast of his wages and the popcorn purchases. He uses humor in explaining his recent decision to swear off "butter topping." Small touches like this are just enough (he's not applying to clown college).
4. Although the writer says he hasn't learned anything at the movies, his essay suggests he has thought carefully about his experience and can write about it clearly and with wit.

Sample 11

I come from a country that is economically oppressed, a country where speaking against the government could cost one his or her life. There is no established government. "Survival of the fittest" is the regulation that we live by. There is no law enforcement, no government to complain to, and no police to call to one's rescue when one is being robbed or attacked.

The average Haitian only completes high school if he or she is fortunate. There exist circumstances in which a student has to leave school to work to care for their family even though work opportunities are insufficient. Times get harder and more unbearable as days go by. People get killed for no fixed reason, food becomes limited, and more and more children are getting ill.

My family consisted of eight people, all living on the second floor of a three-story house that included only two bedrooms. My sister and I slept in the same bed and in the same bedroom as my mother and two aunts. Paying the rent was difficult, for no one in the family was employed.

My grandmother left for the United States in 1988 when I was two years old. Since her arrival in America, she has stayed at someone's house. She was not yet familiar with the language, so it was difficult for her to find a job. She worked as a seamstress at home where she would make dresses for people and get paid, but that was not enough to establish her goal, which was to get her family here in America. Later, she worked as a housekeeper for five years; however, that job was also not sufficient. Knowing that she had children and grandchildren back in her native country, my grandma was determined to do everything in her power to take us out of our misery and bring us here to the land of opportunity.

Although my grandmother was going through harsh and difficult times, like finding transportation for work back and forth in the terrible weather, not being able to communicate with others, or being kicked out, she never forgot about us in Haiti. She would pay our house rent and send money for our schooling and for food. Also she filed for citizenship on our account, so it could be a quicker process of coming to the United States. After seven long years we were able to come to the U.S. November 28, 1995 was such an emotional and joyous day for the entire Joseph family.

There is nothing more that I want in this world than to thank my grandmother and truly show her how important she is to me. She is an exceptional, strong, and independent woman. As of now I am doing my best to attend a four-year college. My love for the community has influenced my career choice. I have resolved in my heart that no matter what I do I must be capable of providing assistance for others. Caring for others has always been my passion and going into a medical field or health profession is what I am striving for. The best way I see fit to give back to a community that has given so much to me is by becoming a nurse practitioner. Hopefully, I will be my grandmother's first grandchild to successfully graduate college. Being able to accomplish all my scholastic goals, I believe, I will not only honor my grandmother but also show her my appreciation for all the hard work she has done for me.

Things to Notice About This Essay

1. This writer gives the reader a strong opening sentence that makes us want to keep reading.

2. The essay describes the author's family but from this the reader can derive a sense of the author's own determination and personality.

3. The essay is well organized, based on the chronology of her grandmother's story, and makes a clear connection between the events of the author's life and her future plans.

4. The essay is quite long; careful editing might keep the important parts and tell the story in fewer words.

5. We learn about the grandmother but it is not the grandmother's generosity, commitment, or love that matter; the reader wants to know more about the author of this essay herself. How did she come to the United States? When did she learn English? How does she live now?

6. What evidence proves that the grandmother's actions have shaped the author's life? You can't borrow someone else's suffering. All essays need proof for the claim; the author's own past (not planned future) actions are the missing pieces in this narration.

Sample 12

A person who influenced me me was Mrs. Baldwin, my best friend's mother. Mrs. Baldwin was always around whenever I went over to see Stacey. She was form Alabama and she always looked up from whatever she was making and said "Hey girl" to me when I came in the kitchen door. I was shocked when my Mom told me that Mrs. Baldwin had cancer. I couldn't believe that anyone I knew, anyone I cared about, could be dying.

It was very hard for everyone as Mrs. Baldwin got sicker. I think her whole family was in shock. She went to the hospital for treatments and for chemotherapy but I knew that things weren't getting better.

Mrs. Baldwin died at home just before Thanksgiving last year. I still think about her often and I know things are completely different for her kids and for her husband. Stacey and I don't ever talk about it but I can tell things have changed.

When Mrs. Baldwin died, I realized that people aren't forever. I know now that we all have to appreciate each other while we can. I think I've changed and I believe that Mrs. Baldwin has had a significant impact on my life. She gave me so much. She gave me a chance to laugh, to tell my stories, and to feel welcomed. She gave me the ability to be myself. Wherever I go, I know that Mrs. Baldwin will be watching over me, helping me to be happy.

Things to Notice About This Essay

1. It is very hard to write about death. Poets and playwrights have been struggling—and often failing—for centuries. Think long and hard before you assign yourself the task of writing in a meaningful and fresh way about illness or death.
2. The essay has a clear focus: Mrs. Baldwin was important to the writer. A bit of specific evidence is offered: the friendly "Hey girl." The reader wonders what other things Mrs. Baldwin did, what conversations they had, what actions created the feelings of warmth and closeness.
3. The writer uses a chronological organization and tells the story toward a conclusion ("I realized . . ."). The essay is organized, but the conclusion isn't completely persuasive. Compare Sample 3 or 9, both of which tell more specific stories to support their conclusions. Remember to show rather than tell.
4. A final version of this essay should include revisions of "completely different," "so much," and "be myself." The reader needs help to visualize what these phrases mean.
5. The writer may have used a spell-checking program, but errors like those in lines one and three show she didn't proofread.

A Final Word

I do not recommend any of these essays to you as models. I present the 12 essays as examples of the strengths (focus, proof, simple language, structure, vividness) and weaknesses that have been discussed throughout this book. It is irrelevant what schools these essays were written for or whether the applicants were accepted. But as an important part of the overall performance and impression of an application, your essay matters. A look at these samples may help you avoid the pitfalls, enjoy the variety, and end up with an essay that gives a connected, strong, and vivid picture of you to the colleges of your choice.

Final Tips

Four Key Points About the Application Essay

1. All the questions, in one way or another, ask the same thing: "Tell us about yourself."

2. So that means you're an authority on the topic.

3. The format is not unfamiliar; it's a regular essay with "you" as the subject.

4. It's not a punishment—it's a chance to add life to your application and to pitch yourself outside the numbers.

Five Myths About Application Essays

1. You have to write about something no one has ever written about before (unlikely and high risk).

2. There's a right answer to every question (there's only your right answer).

3. It's a good idea to be funny or clever or wacky (only if you think they are looking for funny, clever, or wacky applicants).

4. You have to do this alone (every writer asks for feedback, especially in high-stakes settings).

5. Your essay can get you in (only if other credentials also make you an interesting candidate).

Four Common Mistakes

1. Visualizing the admission committee as a bunch of stuffy old professors in tweed jackets and then trying to write something that will impress them.

2. Trying so hard to be memorable that you end up being eccentric.

3. Writing an essay so predictable and generic that with fewer than three noun revisions (change "my Dad" to "my boss," change "summer at the beach" to "summer in the mountains," change the "Mastersingers" to the "varsity basketball team"), this essay could work for most of the senior class.

4. Forgetting that your counselor and your teachers are your allies and that even your parents know something about this topic.

Suggested Reading

Barnet, Sylvan, Marcia Stubbs, and Pat Bellanca. *A Short Guide to College Writing*. 2nd ed. New York: Pearson Longman, 2004.

Corbett, Edward P. J., and Sheryl L. Finkle. *The Little English Handbook: Choices and Conventions*. 8th ed. New York: Pearson Longman, 1998.

Gibaldi, Joseph, and Phyllis Franklin. *MLA Handbook for Writers of Research Papers*. 6th ed. New York: Modern Language Association, 2003.

Hacker, Diana. *A Writer's Reference*. 5th ed. Boston: Bedford Books, 2006.

Roman, Kenneth, and Joseph Raphaelson. *Writing that Works*. 3rd ed. New York: Harper Resources, 2000.

Strunk, William, Jr., and E. B. White. *The Elements of Style*. 4th ed. Boston: Allyn and Bacon Publishers, 2002.

Trimble, John. *Writing with Style: Conversations on the Art of Writing*. 2nd ed. Englewood Cliffs, N.J.: Prentice Hall, Inc., 2000.

Zinsser, William. *On Writing Well, 30th Anniversary Edition: The Classic Guide to Writing Nonfiction*. New York: Harper Resource, 2006.

Preparation for College: From the College Board

College Board. *The College Board Book of Majors* (current edition of biennial publication). New York: The College Board.

College Board. *Guide to Getting Financial Aid* (current edition of annual publication). New York: The College Board.

College Board. *The College Board College Handbook* (current edition of annual publication). New York: The College Board.

College Board. *The Official SAT Study Guide*™. New York: The College Board, 2005.

Schneider, Zola Dincin. *Campus Visits & College Interviews*. 2nd ed. New York: The College Board, 2002.

Note: To order College Board books via the Internet, visit College Board online at www.collegeboard.com.

Index